FRONTIER JUSTICE

Alaska
1898

The Last American Frontier

Ed Ferrell

HERITAGE BOOKS
2007

HERITAGE BOOKS
AN IMPRINT OF HERITAGE BOOKS, INC.

Books, CDs, and more—Worldwide

For our listing of thousands of titles see our website
at
www.HeritageBooks.com

Published 2007 by
HERITAGE BOOKS, INC.
Publishing Division
65 East Main Street
Westminster, Maryland 21157-5026

Other books by the author:
Biographies of Alaska—Yukon Pioneers, 1850-1950
Volumes 1-5
The Dangerous North

International Standard Book Number: 978-0-7884-0881-6

Frontier Justice is dedicated to my son, William Thomas Ferrell, Attorney-at-Law and former police officer.

Contents

ACKNOWLEDGMENTS

Individuals: I would like to express my appreciation to the staff of the Alaska State Library for their help in my research, namely: Debbie Finley, LuAnn Fisher, Patience Frederiksen, B.J. Gardner, Connie Hamann, Susan King, Gladi Kulp, Mike Mitchell, Ron Reed, Kay Shelton, India Spartz, Darren Spence, and Sondra Stanway.

Thanks are also due to Dee Longenbaugh of Observatory Books for allowing me to photograph a 1897 map from her collection to use in *Frontier Justice*.

I want to express my thanks to my wife, Nancy Warren Ferrell, for the many hours she took out from her own busy writing schedule to type, proofread, and to make editorial comments on the manuscript, and to my daughter, Patricia Ferrell, for material on Mollie Walsh.

Photo credits: *Nome Nugget*, September 19, 1902; Alaska State Historical Library: pages 20, 40, 48, 51, 56, 122, 123, 137; Alaska Sportsman, August 1941, page 52; Alaska State Troopers (sketch, 1960), page 104; *Edmonton Journal* (sketch), February 19, 1932, page 112; *The San Francisco Examiner* (sketch), February 8, 1898, page 68. I also appreciate the work of Paul Helmar, Juneau Photo Works, and Art Sutch, Sutch Photography and Digital Imaging.

Story credits: *Edmonton Journal*, February 19, 1932, "Eye Witness Tells Story Last Desperate Stand Trapper Albert Johnson, (Roy Wood, permissions); The Canadian Press for *The Globe* story, January 14, 1932, "Bombs, Rifles, and Posse Fail to Dislodge Hermit from His Cabin-Fortress."(Ms. Ivy Mouland, permissions).

Book credits: I am indebted to the following authors: Dick North, *The Mad Trapper of Rat River* and the sequel, *Trackdown;* Art Petersen and D. Scott Williams, *Murder, Madness, and Mystery, An Historical Narrative of Mollie Walsh Bartlett From the Days of the Klondike Gold Rush;* and Gerald L. Pennington, *Klondike Stampede Register, A Chronology of the Klondike Gold Rush 1897-1898.*

Introduction

The frontier condition which brought about the organization of the vigilantes and the lynch courts in the old west was repeated in the northern gold stampede-- a sudden rush of people of all nationalities into a remote and unsettled territory before the machinery of government and forces of law were put into place. The lawless frontier attracted gunmen, killers, thieves, bunco and sure thing men, and other denizens of the underworld.

Where the law was absent the miners took over. They held court, heard the evidence, and decided on the guilt or innocence of the defendants. Justice was swift. Murderers answered to "Judge Lynch's Court." At least five men are known to have died by the hands of the vigilante courts.

I have selected stories from newspapers and other sources that best reflect frontier justice of the gold rush and early territorial era of Canada and Alaska.

The accounts were typed as originally written, reflecting punctuation, capitalization, spelling, and usage of frontier writers and editors. But, some selections have been edited for clarity, and to move the action along.

Generally, I have used the earliest known account

of an event, but not in all cases. For example, I opted for a 1915 account of the trial and hanging of "Doc" Tanner. It was better written and more detailed than the 1898 story published in *The Seattle Daily Times.* Additionally, the man interviewed for the *Times* article had taken part in the miners' court that tried Tanner. I checked the story against early sources and it agreed in all major details. I titled the story "Hang Me Straight."

For the same reasons, I used an account by J. Carmel published in 1930 of the flogging at Sheep Camp of a thief. Carmel's story was published originally in the Victoria B.C., *Daily News* and reprinted in *The Stroller's Weekly*, November 20, 1930.

I compared his story with *The Skaguay News* [later spelled Skagway] for February 18, 1898 and found it accurate, and better written. I called the story "Sheep Camp Vigilantes."

I have included a selection titled "The Man from the Mountain," an account of Klu-tok, the Indian outlaw. He may have died of natural causes, and was not the victim of frontier justice. But, I believe some trapper or Indian killed Klu-tok and put an end to his murdering rampage. United States Marshal, Stanley Nichols, found the Indian dead in a cabin on the Mulchatana River. His official report stated Klu-tok "died of natural causes as far as I could tell."

By the turn of the century, the miners' courts faded into history. As the law arrived in the camps, justice was not as swift and sure as it had been under the vigilantes. In murder cases, lawyers argued self defense, temporary insanity and any other defense that would benefit their clients. Men that would have been hanged by vigilante courts walked free.

But in 1898, Skagway citizens were in no mood for legal maneuvering. They took over the law to insure justice, the marshal being too friendly with Soapy Smith. A brazen robbery of a Klondiker by Smith's gang sparked the rebellion. A group of armed men, calling themselves "The Committee of 101," warned the gang to leave town or suffer the consequences. In the ensuing confrontation Reid killed Smith, receiving a fatal wound during the shooting.

Vigilantes rounded up gang members and tried them in citizens' courts. Winchester and Colt enforced the decisions. Some of Soapy's men were given prison sentences; others put on boats bound for the Outside. And warned never to return or they would decorate a tree!

On the Canadian side of the border, the "Mounties" maintained law and order. Whitehorse and Dawson never exhibited the lawless character of the American camps. The police enforced the closing of businesses, including saloons on Sunday. When Soapy's men tried to work their scams in Canadian territory, an armed constable escorted them back across the border.

I have tried to follow up on each story. But in some instances, I was unable to find additional information on the event.

This collection was never intended as a historical study, replete with footnotes and bibliography. My purpose was to compile a selection of interesting stories of frontier justice from early day newspapers and other publications.

"There have been thirteen murders committed in the Yukon Territory in thirteen years, all the murderers being convicted and hanged except one, who died before the day set for his execution."

Major S. L. Wood
Royal Canadian Mounted Police

$\mathcal{E}$ager for news from the gold fields, Outside newspapers sometimes fell prey to fanciful yarns made up by Klondikers, or by those claiming to have been in the Klondike. Leo Reid, who related the following George O' Brien story, may fall into the latter category. Reid claimed to have worked the gaming tables in Dawson during its heyday, and saw O'Brien hanged.

George O'Brien and his supposed partner, Graves, killed Fred Clayson, Lynn Relf, and A. Olson in late December 1899, disposing of the bodies in the Yukon River. The bloated corpses surfaced in June. Another body believed to be Graves, was also recovered near Selkirk. Newspapers speculated that O'Brien killed Graves after they had jointly murdered the other three men. And that Graves was killed "...in order to forever silence any dangerous testimony he might give...."

George O'Brien died on the gallows in Dawson City, August 23, 1901.

Reid's narrative appeared in the *Dawson Daily News*, June 9, 1911.

DAWSON'S SERIAL KILLER

A few days ago the historic jail building--the old Dawson police barracks--was torn down, and now the spot of ground is open to public view where stood the scaffold from which O'Brien, Fournier, Labelle, Elfors, and other Yukon murderers were swung into eternity. In that same spot also was buried the remains of a number of the murderers, among them those of O'Brien. Quick lime was thrown on the bodies at the time of burial. The denouement of the Klondike hangman's half acre, and recollections of O'Brien and others there planted comes about, singularly enough, just at the time of receipt from

New York of a peculiar yellow yarn spun by an alleged former Yukoner.

Now comes the story reputed to have been told in a New York cafe by one Leo Reid, said to have been an early-day Dawson gambler. He claims to have been on the trail and to have traded for O'Brien's dog, and to have been in Dawson with the dog after the murder. One dog is known to have figured in the trial, but not in the way told by Reid. Reid claims O'Brien's partner was Ed Wilson. The name is a new one to Dawson in connection with the case. The story by Reid as published in a New York paper is written by Dave Clark, and is as follows:

"During the rush to the gold country grafters from everywhere got in the van and tailed along. Men that could have made plenty of money on the square, if they wanted to, thought they could get it easier by matching their wits with their more fortunate brothers. O'Brien was one of that class.

"He would commit murder rather than work, if he had to go to extremes. He had gone into Dawson with the one idea of getting money with the least trouble. They had not been in Dawson a month when they got into trouble with the police, so they had to lay low for a while.

"People were coming out with gold and currency, from Dawson to Skagway. To get the boat, they had to travel overland nearly 600 miles of wilderness with dog teams.

"O'Brien decided to camp along the trail and wait for the more prosperous ones and relieve them of their wealth. About 200 miles out of Dawson there was a water hole that was open all winter, a short distance back from the trail. There was some brush near it, so O'Brien and his gang decided to camp there. They had a dog team and a horse and sleigh.

"Big Ed Wilson, one of the partners took the dog team, after they were settled in camp, and returned to Dawson. He was to inform O'Brien when there was a prospector coming along that would make it worth their while to 'stick up.' In that way they took no unnecessary chances and worked over two months without being tipped off. Their system was to wait until Ed reached the camp with the information as to who was coming out, how much they had, how many in the party, etc., then O'Brien and partner would stick them up when they reached the camp; kill them and throw their bodies in the water hole. At times they would make a mistake, and hold up the wrong party, but they had to be killed just the same to keep from tipping O'Brien off. They knew that the first man that got away would spread the news and they would be caught and killed themselves, so they took no chances.

"About this time I decided to leave San Francisco and go to Dawson to open a gambling house. I knew that the claims were all staked out, so a game of chance was the next best thing. I had quite a bank roll at the time I made my start. I bought the best outfit I could get in Skagway and started over the 600 miles that separate it from Dawson.

"I made a few stops at different camps to rest myself and dogs and then started again. On the last leg of my journey, I happened to put up at O'Brien's camp. I was treated very well and was invited to stay as long as I wanted to. I tarried long enough to give the dogs a good rest, and then told O'Brien I was going to make a fresh start.

"It seems that he and his partner were preparing to make their getaway about the time I arrived, and I suppose they were too busy to bother about me. But I was going in, and as very few people have money take into a mining camp, they didn't bother me. They thought I was going to prospect. They had over $60,000 in gold then, but they had been 'tipped off,' I found out afterward, and only thought of their liberty.

"Just before I left their camp they offered to swap a dog for some grub. Dogs were scarce at the time, so I took the dog and gave them some flour and bacon. The dog nearly caused me spending a winter in jail, incidentally.

"It seems that a party that owned one of the best claims there was coming on with about eighty thousand in gold and currency, and had been stuck up. Ed had been in a few days before and tipped them off, and then went back to Dawson without waiting for the party to reach the camp. In fact, he never waited; he always played safe.

"When the party arrived they were covered from O'Brien's camp and ordered to throw up their hands and back up which they refused to do, opening fire on O'Brien and his partner, but two of them were killed after a fight and the third one got away with the dog team and gold. O'Brien followed with the horse and sleigh, but could not overtake the dogs in the snow. A horse in that part of the country is not a very useful animal, as the heavy animal breaks through the snow crust. Dogs, being light, keep on the surface.

"After a few miles of pursuit O'Brien decided it was useless to try to overtake the prospector, so returned to camp and made preparations to get away. They knew as soon as the escaping prospector reached Skagway, the news would be flashed back to Dawson and they would have very little chance of getting out then.

"The fellow that got away must have passed me on the trail, but I suppose I was stopping over at one of the camps at the time he passed. After I arrived in Dawson I found that most every one in town knew the dog I had with my team belonged to O'Brien. It was a very conspicuous animal and had been picked up by O'Brien in Skagway when he was going to Dawson.

"When I arrived the town was burning up with the talk of O'Brien and his partners. I had put up my own team and was looking around the town when I spied an old pal of mine from Frisco, Al Hoyle. Of course, I was tickled to death to see him, and we talked about the country and the best part of town to open up in.

"After I told what I intended doing there. It was then for the first time that I discovered how lucky I was in meeting him. He told me the story of O'Brien, and wanted to know if I had seen anything of him on my way in. I gave him an account of my movements from the time I left Skagway and explained the dog incident. He was then sure I had stayed at O'Brien's camp. I took him over to where I had put the team up and showed him the dog.

"Al recognized the dog immediately and advised me to turn it out as soon as possible, as they would hold me as a witness against O'Brien if they found that I had met him at the trail. You know in that part of the country they keep you in jail until they hold circuit court in the spring. So I would have to stay in about as long as you would get here in the East for a stick-up.

"I got rid of the dog, all right, but it was no easy matter. I want to tell you, as no one wanted it, being aware that it was O'Brien's. To start with, I couldn't get the dog to leave my camp after it had been fed, and I had to take it to the other end of the town at midnight, tie it up and run away.

"As soon as it got noised around that O'Brien's dog had been found, they thought he himself was in town, and the mounted police started to look for him, with the dog as a guide. I had to stay under cover while the search was going on for fear I would meet them and the dog would recognize me and tip it off. Of course, their hunt for O'Brien in Dawson was futile. Mounted police from Skagway and Dawson started over the trail looking for him, but it wasn't long after that we received the news they had him.

"The White Mountain Trail Railroad company was building a line over Chilkoot pass, between Dawson and Skagway, to save the climb over the mountain. They did not have it finished, but the cut was open to people on foot. If your team was loaded, you could walk over the cut and save the dogs the extra weight and meet them when they arrived on the other side.

"Teams had to take the roundabout way to get to the other end of the trestle, and it was there O'Brien was caught, five Northwestern Mounted Police covering him as he came around the cut he had walked over. He refused to say anything about his partner at the time he was arrested, but on the stand at his trial he told how he had walked over the trestle and given his partner the horse. That he said was the last time he saw his partner, but it was the consensus of opinion in Dawson that O'Brien having the money, killed his partner to keep from cutting it up with him. Neither the partner nor the horse and sleigh were ever heard of afterward.

"After O'Brien was sentenced to be hung the police tried to get him to make a statement as to who his partners were, but he refused to say anything about the case. Ed Wilson, the partner that was in Dawson, went up to Gold Hill as soon as the news arrived of O'Brien's capture and came out, only to be lodged in jail there. The night before Dawson received the news of the arrest he had been in the Monte Carlo, and from what I heard cleaned up $2000 playing the 'bank.' If he did he was the only one to finish with anything. He was reported in Skagway, waiting for the boat out.

"Just before O'Brien paid the penalty the police asked him who his victims were, in the hope that the money taken from him could be divided among their nearest relatives, but his answer was: 'I don't know who they were, and I don't care.'

"At the time he died in 1898, there had been reported missing over seventy-five people. And O'Brien was supposed to have killed most of them. There was no way to recover the bodies, as the victims were washed into the Yukon.

"Three life prisoners were used to kill him, and by an ingenious method that kept them from knowing which one of the three had released the trap. It consisted of three strings--one attached to the weight. At a given signal the three strings were cut and the trap dropped. The prisoners used in that capacity never were allowed to see the scaffold.

"I was one of the spectators at O'Brien's trial, but was not called as a witness, as he failed to recognize me, and no one but my friend Al Hoyle, and O'Brien knew of the dog transaction. I never saw a man take a sentence with the indifference that he took his. He walked to the scaffold with the step of a man about to make a speech."

AFTERWARD: George O'Brien was buried in Dawson in an unmarked grave. As Clayson's body passed through town on the way south for burial, the Arctic Brotherhood gave him a funeral. *The Daily Alaskan* described the rite as " ... one of the largest ever held in Skagway." Fred Clayson had served on the first city council in Skagway and was well known.

Edward Clayson contested his son's will. Fred had left his estate to Willam Clayson, a brother to distribute the property to the family. Samuel Lovell, an attorney in Skagway who drew up the will shortly before Fred Clayson's murder, told *The Alaskan* that the will was executed for the sole purpose of depriving Edward Clayton of any of the property of the deceased. In conference with Lovell, Clayton remarked:"...He [the father] has forced my mother and the children to earn a living ever since I can remember, squandered it, giving them nothing in return but abuse and brutality."

FRED HARDY

This sketch of Fred Hardy appeared in *The Nome Nugget* in the September 19, 1902 edition.

Fred Harvey was the first legally executed criminal in Alaska. Prior to his death, vigilante courts administered justice on the northern frontier. The earliest recorded vigilante lynching occurred in Wrangell in the 1870s. As late as the spring ? of 1900, Lituya Bay miners hanged Martin Servert for murdering Steve Fredigo, an employee of the Lituya Bay Gold Mining Company.

$\mathcal{B}$orn in Lexington, Ohio in 1876, Frederick E. Watkins, adopted the surname Hardy, his stepfather's name. He resided in Lexington until 1897, working as a telegraph operator. In 1897, he enlisted in the Second U.S. Cavalry at Columbus. Stationed at various camps, he eventually shipped to the Philippines, reaching the islands in September of 1898. Hardy claimed he held the rank of second lieutenant in the First Tennessee Volunteer Regiment. In the service, he was known as "Diamond Dick," after a character in the dime novels he liked to read.

Mustered out at the Presidio, San Francisco in late March 1901, Hardy left for Alaska on the schooner *Arago*. While ashore on Unimak Island, he deserted the ship. Shortly after, in early June, Hardy and a companion [?] murdered three prospectors. The story of Fred Hardy's last days was carried in *The Nome Nugget* in the September 19, 1902 edition.

HANGMAN'S JUSTICE

The crime for which Hardy paid the death penalty was committed on Unimak Island on June 7, 1901. The Sullivan brothers were first shot down like dogs, and a shot fired at P.J. Rooney broke his leg. He attempted to escape with Owen Jackson who was also a member of the party, but fell to the ground where another shot from the killer's rifle ended his life. The story of the murders as told by Owen Jackson at the trial at Unalaska, September 7 is as follows:

"We came down to Cape Lapin about 11:00 on June 6, 1901, and came ashore and unloaded our stuff. We put up a tent and put the goods in it, had lunch and started back for the balance of our stuff to where it had been landed from the schooner *Lizzie Colby.*

"We had our dinner and left there at 1 o'clock and started back up about 20 miles to where we moved part of the goods from. We expected to come back that night. When we got ashore it was a pretty bad place to land; and the surf was pretty bad. We left the boat about a half mile further down. We packed our stuff down to it so that we could get it the next morning.

"The next morning we started down for Cape Lapin; we got there about 11:30 o'clock. When we were coming in Rooney hollered: 'There is two men going up the creek with our packs.' I looked around and saw only one man. My back was to him. I was rowing; Con Sullivan was in the bow of the boat and hollered: 'Pull quick. The tent is down and everything is gone.'

"We pulled in quick and found that there was not a single thing left there. Three of us started up the creek in that direction. We saw the men going, Rooney being left in charge of the boat. Florence Sullivan went to the cabin, and Con and I went on down to the beach. I wanted to see if I could see a dory. I searched half an hour and me and Con came and we met Florence at the cabin.

"Then we started up the creek and Florence went the other way to a little island, where we next saw him, and Con said, 'There's Florence.' I looked around and saw him and about a quarter of a minute after that the shooting commenced. Four shots went off, but we could not see any smoke; four shots were fired, when a man stood up from behind a rock. His back was to us, and he saw us and went on toward where we saw Florence, but he was gone. We did not know who would be shot next. We went down to the creek as fast as we could.

"When we got near the boat, Rooney hollered, 'Come boys, let's get out to sea.' He then started hollering about poor Florence. Then we ran to the boat and hardly got our hands on it, when a shot came and hit Rooney in the leg. I said, 'Drop behind the boat.' They were firing into the boat. Rooney hollered, ' I'm shot.' We laid down behind the boat and Con said, 'We will have to make a break; we will be all killed.'

"I said, 'We will have to do it quick.' I no more than said this when a bullet struck the boat. We got up and both went toward the bluff. We had not gone more than fifteen or twenty yards when Con was shot between the shoulders.

"He threw up his hands and hollered, 'Oh Lord, oh, Lord,' as loud as he could.

"I went on and the next shot I got hit in the leg. I looked around and saw Con lying on the beach. The bullets were flying around me and I could hear them hitting the rocks behind me. I went as far as I could until the ocean cut me off. I stayed there until I saw Rooney coming around the point. He kept coming on and finally lay down and beckoned to me. I went over and said, 'Pat, for God's sake, pick up courage and let's try to get out of here.'

"He said, 'There's no use; we are going to be all killed; he is over there now searching Con's pockets.' Then I told him again, 'For God's sake, pick up courage and come.' But he shook his head. Then I made a break and started climbing the cliff. I managed to get up to it and stayed there until after Rooney was killed. I must have stayed there twenty minutes or so, when I heard two shots in quick succession again. When the second shots were fired, I took off my gum boots and started off. I kept going day and night. I traveled all that evening and the next day and I struck a cabin about 11:00 at night.

"The next morning when I was ready to start, I saw natives coming up, I bolted the door. One of them tried to enter and another got on the roof and looked down and said, 'How do.' I made for an axe and stayed there for three days. I then started for False Pass and wandered around until I reached Scott's camp."

[*The Nome Nugget* then continued with the story

15

of the arrest and trial of Hardy]

Fred Hardy was arrested on July 23 [1901] on Unimak Island by U.S. Deputy Marshal O'Sullivan of Unalaska. He was stopping at a lodging house. In a closet, he saw Hardy secrete a nugget pin, and a gold watch in a leather pouch, and some other articles, which were subsequently recovered. Found with him was a rifle, two razors, about $600 in currency and other articles which were identified at the trial as the property of the Sullivan brothers.

Hardy asserted that after he left the *Arago,* he traveled inland and found three men in a cabin. One was called Jack, another Jim and he didn't remember the name of the third. They had money, rifles and a lot of other articles, and when he expressed some curiosity as to where the men had gotten all those things, they told him they had made a "catch." These men were staying at Charley Rosenberg's cabin, according to Fred Hardy's statement, and they told him they had left the schooner *Dove.*

At the trial it was conclusively proven that Rosenberg himself had occupied the cabin at the time Hardy stated he had met the three strangers there.

Hardy's trial began on Sept. 2, 1901, at Unalaska, before Judge Wickersham. It ended on Sept. 7 where the jury returned a verdict of murder in the first degree.

Hardy was sentenced to be hanged at Nome on Dec. 6 last, but a new trial having been denied an appeal was taken to the United States supreme court. On June 2, 1902, the supreme court affirmed the judgment of the lower court, and on July 18 Hardy was again sentenced by Judge Moore to be hanged on Sept. 19, 1902.

Hardy's last day on earth was spent very much as have all the other days since he has been confined. He maintained his usual cheerfulness and good nature for, as a prisoner, Hardy gave little trouble.

Yesterday he expressed a desire to make his will. United States Marshal Richards, who has left nothing undone for Hardy's comfort, accommodated Hardy, and Guy Brubecker, a stenographer and notary in the marshal's office, drew the will. In it Hardy disposed of his personal effects and 320 acres of land, which, he said, he owned in the south.

Marshal Richards has been very kind to Hardy, as have all the jail officials. Yesterday he said to the marshal: "You have been very kind to me, kinder than my own father, and I won't fail you tomorrow; that's all that I can do for you." To the editor of the *Nugget*, who visited Hardy last night, he expressed himself in similar terms, thanking him for kindness shown.

Hardy asked Deputy Marshal Estabrook last night if he would not be permitted to tie the knot about his own neck. Mr. Estabrook told him no, as the knot had been already tied, tried, and twisted. Hardy remarked that no man about to be hanged had ever tied his own knot, and he would like to have that distinction. "I like the way you talk to me," replied Hardy, "you've been frank with me, and that's what I like."

Last night he played a game of checkers with Guard D'Hierry, and he played well, keeping his mind on the game and making few errors. When the *Nugget* representative visited his cell at 10 o'clock he was cheerful. With W.A. Miller, who also called, he discussed rifle shooting and how, at 500 yards in five shots, he had hit the bulls eye every time.

Then he talked of his approaching death and said he would be cool on the scaffold; he affirmed his innocence with his usual calmness and he said he would make a speech on the scaffold, but he didn't know how long it would be, though he had it all arranged in his head. As the *Nugget* man went down the steps leading from Hardy's cell the strains of "Home Sweet Home," played by Hardy on a harmonica, followed him and filled the entire jail. Hardy asked Mrs. Mary F. Hart, who called to see him, if she had ever heard the song called "Goo-Goo Eyes?" She answered yes. "I wrote it," said Hardy.

There is a belief about the jail that Hardy's mind was shattered. Hardy retired shortly after 12 last night but his sleep was restless for some time. Finally he fell into peaceful slumber and slept until about 6:30 when he was aroused by the death watch. He dressed himself carefully and combed his hair with usual care. He wore a black suit and black negligee sateen shirt with a tie. The sister of Holy Cross Hospital called shortly afterwards and administered religious consolation. On his left breast Hardy wore a large cross.

At 7:30 Rev. Father Cataldo called and the sacrament was administered. Later Hardy ate his breakfast, which consisted of veal chops, boiled eggs, potatoes, toast and coffee, which he seemed to enjoy.

As the bell in the school building clanged the hour of nine, Marshal Richards read the death warrant to Hardy in his cell. Hardy leaned against the cell calmly smoking a cigarette. At the close, tears were in his eyes.

"That all?" asked Hardy in a husky voice as the reading of the warrant ended.

"That is all," said the marshal.

Then he said, "What time is the thing coming off? Right away?"

"Yes," said the marshal.

Five minutes later the little procession to the gallows started. Marshal Richards led the way, followed by Hardy supported by a guard on either side, while another followed behind: then came Father Cataldo and a number of jail officials. Hardy mounted the scaffold with a firm step. He was placed on the trap by Deputy Estabrook, his arms and legs were strapped, the black cap was place on his head, but was not pulled down.

"You have anything to say, Fred Hardy?" asked Mr. Estabrook. Hardy said yes, and he began a rambling speech which lasted fully ten minutes. His voice broke at times, but withal, he maintained wonderful composure. He protested his innocence to the last, saying that he was not guilty of murder: he had but a few minutes to live and he wanted the spectators who filled the body of the building to know that he was innocent, and that he died a Christian with malice toward none.

He paid the tribute to the kindness of the officials, naming each one. Two or three times he hesitated, and Father Cataldo and Deputy Estabrook helped him out with his words. "I'll bid you all a long good bye," were his last words. Quickly the black cap was drawn over his face and the rope adjusted. Deputy Estabrook gave signs, the trap was sprung, by whom no one probably will ever know, the body shot downward, Fred Hardy was hanged at 9:40 o'clock this morning. He died without flinching, protesting his innocence with his latest breath, his body never quivered, his neck being broken

Dr. Hill felt the pulse and Dr. White examined the heart, and life was pronounced extinct in exactly 9 minutes and 48 seconds. The body was then cut down and an inquest held, the jury returning the usual verdict. Fred Hardy had paid the penalty for his crime.

AFTERWARD: Fred Hardy was the only man ever charged with the murders on Unimak Island. Owen Jackson testified that shots came from two different directions. When authorities examined the scene of the shooting, they found empty rifle cartridges in the spots Jackson indicated. George Aston, also a deserter from the *Arago*, was taken into custody but released. He claimed he met Hardy after the murders.

The *Nome News* for August 7, 1901 asked the rhetorical question: "Did Hardy have a partner in the shooting and then kill him, taking all the spoils himself?" Only Hardy knew the answer, and he took it to the gallows. His story has a strange, supernatural ending. See "Hanged Man's Ghost."

MARY GIBSON HART

In 1900, when the gold excitement was at its height in Alaska, she was sent as correspondent by a number of journals to the Nome goldfields. In addition to her writing, Hart engaged in mining with indifferent success. While working as a reporter for *The Nome Nugget*, she experienced an encounter with the supernatural-- executed murderer Fred Hardy returned to haunt her.

$\mathcal{M}$ary Hart was a remarkable woman in a man's world--the Alaska-Yukon Frontier. During the gold rush era, she homesteaded, mined, mushed dogs in the wildest parts of Alaska. Hart represented the North at the world's expositions in Seattle, St.Louis and Portland. For a number of years, she worked as a reporter for the *Nome Nugget*. Shortly before Fred Hardy's execution, she interviewed the condemned man and, unknowingly unleashed forces from another world. Mary Hart's account appeared in the *Nugget*, June 2, 1916.

HANGED MAN'S GHOST

Dread of a hanged man's ghost prevents Mrs. Mary E. Hart, Alaska's leading woman citizen, from ever returning to Nome.

"Until now, I have always been afraid to tell why I can never go back to Nome," she began. "People today can't credit experiences such as I am about to relate.

"It grew out of my unwilling part in the first legal execution in the Territory, the hanging of Fred Hardy, a youth convicted of murdering three prospectors at Dutch Flat. I was then reporting for a Nome paper and had been assigned to cover the execution and try for a confession from Fred Hardy, although he steadily maintained his innocence.

"Having won his confidence and all hope for a reprieve being gone, I believed Hardy would admit his guilt to me at the last if he was the murderer. He had but a few hours to live when I spoke to him through the bars of his cell in the old Nome icehouse.

"'Mrs. Hart,'" he said, 'do you believe in life after death: do you think the dead can make themselves manifest to the living? 'I do,' he continued, 'and shall return to tell you about death and about the beyond--if I will be welcome.'"

"Yes," I stammered with creeping horror, "Yes,

21

you will be welcome, Fred." What else could I have said to a boy about to die?

"I was in my office writing the story of the hanging which I had witnessed. It was quiet and I was alone.

"And then Fred Hardy, whom I had seen dashed into eternity, came back--to haunt me for many hideous weeks.

"I sat rigid in my chair, unable to move or speak. It was as though I were being choked to death; as if I were undergoing what that twenty-one year old youth must have experienced during his last moment. I am confident I would have died but for an interruption.

"A girl we knew as Sunshine knocked at the door, entered, touched me on the shoulder, shrieked, 'My God, Hardy is here' and fell to the floor alternately fainting and hysterical. She spoke in Hardy's voice, describing death torments-- Sunshine who had witnessed the hanging, speaking in Hardy's low, peculiar voice. It was frightful beyond words.

"That almost lethal paralysis left my body at the instant Sunshine touched my shoulder, but from that day until I left Nome, I was haunted day and night by that inexplicable presence. I make no attempt to explain this ghastly experience. But I shall never return to Nome, because I am afraid."

In the winter of 1896, an argument over a ten cent beer at the Douglas City Hotel set off one of the deadliest man hunts in Alaska's history. The details of the trouble between William Birch and Henry Osborne are not clear, but in the ensuing fight, Osborne came out the winner. Later at the Standard Saloon, the fight broke out again. Joseph and Robert Birch jumped into the fray. During the fight, Slim bit off Osborne's nose and part of an ear. The three Birch brothers were arrested and indicted for mayhem.

The jury found Joseph not guilty. But, Robert, found guilty of assault and battery, was sentenced to 10 months in jail and fined $ 350. As for William the jury deadlocked. Later the court retried and sentenced him to three years at San Quentin. Before being transferred south, masked men overpowered Lindquist, the jailer, and set Birch free. Birch and his cohorts fled to Admiralty Island.

The January 27, 1897 and February 1897 issues of the *Mining Record* carried the story of the man hunt.

BEAR CREEK SHOOT OUT

The story of the crime, trial and sentence of William T. alias "Slim" Birch is yet fresh in the minds of our readers and his escape from jail has barely ceased to be the talk of the town. Now it is overshadowed by the tragic events which have grown out of it. The affair has passed down the gamut of crime each blacker than the preceding , through assault, mayhem and jail breaking and now murder. He is a hunted fugitive in the snow-clad hills of Admiralty Island.

Since the escape of Slim Birch from the Juneau jail

23

the officers and their deputies have been tireless in their search for him. They discover the fugitive had found shelter in a cabin on Admiralty Island, about two miles from the beach. The steamer *Lucy* was chartered and started at 11 o'clock a.m. Saturday to undertake the capture of the desperados. Marshall William Hale was in charge of the posse with deputy William Watt, A.A. Bays, William D. Lindquist, and Indian policeman, Sam Johnson.

The marshal and his deputies arrived on the boat *Lucy* Sunday morning, disembarking on the beach nearest the cabin in which Birch had taken refuge. The party proceeded some two miles up the creek until they came in sight of the cabin. Confident that no resistance would be offered,. Hale, Watt, and Bays approached the door. One of them rapped for admittance.

Without warning they were fired upon, through the closed door, a storm of bullets singing past them. Almost immediately the door opened and a second volley fired. One of the shots hit Bays, passing through his thigh and inflicting a painful flesh wound. Hale and his companions ran for shelter afforded by trees.

As the firing continued through portholes cut in the cabin, the posse gradually withdrew to better shelter and returned the fire. Watt had partially concealed himself behind the roots of a fallen tree, where he was joined by Hale. Watt had been struck by a bullet which had broken his leg in two places. Bays, wounded, was sent back to the beach to secure help and the fight continued, lasting in all from the time of the first volley for fully an hour without seeming advantage to either side.

Meanwhile Birch and one of his companions had slipped from the cabin and gained the hillside above the scene whence from different points they began and continued a rapid rifle fire upon the posse. At length a bullet struck Marshal Hale in the left side above and back of the hip, passing downward and to the front, disabling him for further activity in the affray. Hale was knocked or threw himself over the creek bank and painfully crawled toward the beach. The Indian policeman who had seen Hale fall over the bank, dodged around and joined him, assisting him toward the boat. Before reaching the beach they met Captain Yorke and the wounded marshal was taken aboard and cared for as well as was possible. Lindquist unable to render aid, had also returned to the beach. Captain York steamed to Juneau with the wounded men and for reinforcements.

At 4:30 Sunday evening the steamer *Lucy's* shrill whistle sounded its alarm as under full steam she came plowing across the channel. Citizens hastened to the ferry float. The news spread like wildfire through the city and steps were taken to organize a posse to capture the desperadoes. Captain William Martin selected nineteen men of known integrity. The steamer *Rustler* started at 8:20 Sunday evening, steaming direct to the mouth of Bear creek.

After a run of four hours and fifteen minutes, the signal for half speed was sounded in the engine room and a few minutes later was followed by the signal for the engineer to bring his boat to a stop. We had arrived about 200 yards off shore along the northern part of Admiralty island. The lights were still out and the anchor was not dropped. The captain of the volunteers in the after part of the boat gave the order to "load arms," and then followed the ominous click, click as cartridges were loaded into magazines of the Winchesters.

Silently the heavy shore boat was brought around to the side door of the steamer and landed the posse on shore. We tramped over the treacherous ice and snow, finally bringing up at Bear creek.

On the beach a half mile above the creek we discovered the cabin of the prospectors who had refused help to Marshal Hale when he was returning in his wounded condition to the boat. Captain Martin, suspectting the occupants of the cabin of being accomplices of "Slim" Birch, ordered his men to surround the house. The two miners within were suddenly roused from their slumbers as the door of their cabin was broken in. Captain Martin satisfied himself that the men were not in any way connected with the Birch gang. He then commanded one of the men, J.F. McWilliams, to get up and dress and to then lead the way to the cabin, near which the unfortunate deputy marshal was supposed to be lying.

In single file we started along the trail that had been travelled over by Marshal Hale and posse about sixteen hours before. For most of the distance, the trail led over very level ground covered with from two to four feet of snow and generally through a scanty, scrubby growth of timber. Several times it became necessary to carry a lighted lantern in order to keep upon the beaten path.

At about a quarter to four, while it was still quite dark, we arrived in close proximity to the cabin. About 100 feet ahead of us we could but dimly see the outlines of a small log hut. A stop was made to reconnoiter. Several times Captain Martin hollered to learn if there was anyone within the hut. As there was no response to the call the order was given to fire three rounds into the house. Still there was no reply and then an order was given to scatter and rush the hut.

Immediately the lantern was again brought into service and a search was made for Marshal Watt. The search did not last long; the lifeless remains of the brave officer were found about a hundred and fifty yards from the cabin. He was lying upon his back and was frozen stiff; his right hand was clinched and rested upon his breast; his left hand was also tightly closed but the arm extended straight out from the body. By his side with the muzzle sticking deep in the snow stood his empty rifle, as if one of his last thoughts had been to mark the spot where he lay, that the rescuing party which he knew would come might the more readily find his lifeless body. Everything indicated very plainly that the last moments of the officer's life were painful ones.

His eyes were wide open and were covered with a thin layer of ice; his teeth were tightly clenched, but his lips were open and in every drawn or contorted feature something seemed to mutely protest the sufferings of the victim in his last moments. Watt had been shot two times; evidently the first shot struck him about midway in the back of the left thigh, the bullet ranging downward and coming out at the knee cap; the second bullet, which in all probability was the immediate cause of death, probably struck him while he was crawling away; it entered the left of him, seemingly taking an upward course and lodging somewhere in the body. Watt's body lay at the very edge of the little stream that at one point passes close by the house, his wounded leg, the bone of which had been badly shattered, was twisted, but extended in rigid condition over the water. A few feet away a deep imprint in the hard snow showed where the dying man had lain for some time. All around the body the snow was dyed with blood.

A watch was stationed outside the cabin and the volunteers crowded into a little 12 x 14 foot room that had lately been occupied by the murderers, to await the coming of daylight. A fire was kindled in the stove and then a search was made among the piles of stuff in the room for articles that might be used for purposes of identification.

The fugitives had left behind them enough provisions to have lasted them many days. Two wide bunks extended along one end of the room and they were liberally supplied with good blankets. All this we burned or destroyed before quitting the cabin.

The floor of the cabin was liberally scattered with empty rifle shells; there were two sizes, 38-90 and 45-70. On one side of the house was a door and on the opposite side was a window; at the front end a loophole three feet in length had been made by cutting away a chink from between two logs that were close under the low roof.

About ten feet from the front end of the house and directly in front of the loophole stands a large tree fully nine feet in circumference. It was behind this tree that Hall, Watt and Lindquist first sought shelter from the fusillade that was suddenly poured upon them. Bays, who had been wounded at the first fire, from the doorway of the cabin ran to a smaller tree a few yards away and a little to the left of the cabin.

To the right of the cabin, about eighty yards, on a low hill are the trees from behind which "Slim" Birch poured his deadly fire. Birch succeeded in slipping from the house unseen, and running along the edge of the first ridge managed by a circuitous route to get to his point of deadly action without the knowledge of the officers. The first intimation the latter had of their new danger was when the shots commenced to come from that direction and when Birch cried "You will try to catch Slim Birch, will you?"

Bays, bleeding profusely, had already left the tree behind which he had sought shelter and ran for assistance towards the boat. Watt ran from the big tree to a small fallen tree that was lying with its roots in the air. The tree was rotten and crumbly and afforded no protection from the bullets. Hale fled from the tree behind which he first hid and stopped to exchange shots with Birch from behind the tree where Bays had lately knelt, but as he was then subjected to severe cross fire from the loopholes in the cabin and from Birch, he next ran to the fallen tree where Watt had endeavored to find some protection. Hale found Watt to be badly wounded and it was while he was stooping over to examine the wound in Watt's leg that he too received a bullet which struck him in the left side above the back of the hip. The bullet was evidently fired from the window of the cabin. Lindquist remained behind the big tree for some minutes after the other two officers had left, and the numerous bullet marks bear evidence of the miraculous escape the jailer must have had.

Almost a half dozen feet back from the upturned roots behind which Watt and Hale had both been shot was a miniature fall in the creek bed. Hale staggered back after receiving his wound and fell over this drop into the water. Watt dragged himself around the stream, leaving a trail of blood behind him to the spot where his lifeless remains were found.

Lindquist and Hale and the native who accompanied the posse had now fled and tracks that the rescuing party followed up with the coming of daylight told a story.

It was plainly evident that as soon as the shooting ceased, the murderous outlaws hurriedly gathered a few things together and departed leaving a trail behind them leading in a southerly direction. "Slim" Birch did not return to the cabin, but kept along the ridge of the hill for nearly half a mile where his trail led down to the canyon and his footsteps were merged with those of his guilty comrades.

It was evident from the footprints that there were but four men in the party that traveled southward. It was suspected by Captain Martin that the desperadoes were headed for Green bay, where possibly a boat awaited them and with the intention of hastening to that place the volunteers, taking with them the remains of the late marshal, hastened back to the *Rustler*, only to learn upon arriving there that there was not enough coal upon the boat to steam to that point. Nothing remained for the disconsolate little party but to steam back to Juneau to be more properly equipped.

[The February 3, 1897 *Mining Record* carried the story of the capture of Birch and Schell]

The party which left here last Monday on the *Rustler* reached Bear creek and at an early hour Tuesday morning and unloaded twenty men, the remainder of the posse steamed to Green's bay. Going at once to the outlaw's cabin, they took up Birch's trail and following it through the snow to Green's bay. They found the *Rustler*

29

awaiting their arrival. Then it was learned that an Indian had seen Birch and one companion. The night was spent aboard the boat. The next morning the cabins at Green's bay were surrounded and entered, but the fugitives had taken to the woods. The posse instituted a rigid search of the vicinity, just before 9 o'clock a.m. an Indian found the two fugitives lying between two logs, covered by a blanket.

The Indian gave a signal to R.L. Cheney and L.H. Olsen who were nearby. Cheney returned to the cabin and notified the posse members who immediately went to his assistance. In the mean time Olsen remained on the sport with rifle in hand in case the murders should awaken.

On the arrival of the other men, Cheney and Olsen sprang on the sleeping desperados. Contrary to expectations little or no resistance was made; the fugitives were in fact worn out by hunger and exposure. Then it was discovered that Birch's companion was Hiram Schell who had robbed Treadwell Mining company and sentenced to a year's imprisonment in the jail at Sitka.

Birch took the capture rather coolly, and tried to use a revolver which was quickly wrested from him. He glanced at Olsen, whom he recognized and remarked "Hello Pete, I'm glad to see somebody here I know." The prisoners' were secured with cords and were taken aboard the *Rustler*. Here they were unbound but guarded by four men. Birch was always watching to seize a weapon whenever anyone passed near him, but the opportunity was not afforded him. The prisoners were transferred to the steamer *Seaolin* and secured with iron manacles.

Birch commented," it's a good thing they caught me asleep." He did not know he had killed Watt, but was aware that some of the posse had been struck by his fire. He cracked jokes about his irons being rather rough jewelry, and remarked that he would rather die than spend three years in San Quentin. He said he would have shot Lindquist but a fragment of icicle struck by a bullet had hit him on the arm numbing it

The prisoners were poorly clad and without provisions except for a piece of venison they had stolen from an Indian. They threatened to kill him if he did not canoe them across Green bay. Just then the *Rustler* came in sight and the outlaws ran into the woods where they were later captured. The prisoners were taken aboard the *Pinta*, an United States Navy gun boat.

AFTERWARD: This story has an unbelievable twist. When Birch and Schell stood trial in Sitka, the jury acquitted them of the murder charges. *The Alaskan* [Sitka] printed a special edition covering the trial. Unfortunately copies of that date are missing. However, the December 11, 1898, edition of *The Alaskan* printed Judge C.S. Johnson's charge to the jury. From this, it is apparent Birch's lawyer argued self defense. And Schell claimed Birch forced him at gun point to take part in the Bear Creek shooting.

In an editorial, the Sitka paper observed that the U.S. Attorney had difficulty in finding witnesses to the murder of Marshal Watt. This was the reason the government lost the case. In those days, Alaska had a fluid population and the key witnesses had moved on.

. The posse said it found the tracks of four men at the Bear Creek cabin. If so, the men were never identified. Marshal Hale and Bays recovered from their wounds. *The Alaskan* gave credit to Sam Johnson, the Indian policeman, for keeping up a covering fire while the men withdrew from the deadly cross fire that Birch and Schell [?] poured out on them from the ridge.

There is no further record of the Birch brothers. Slim and Robert still had jail time to serve for the mayhem charge.

ALASKA
Mining Record

VOLUME VIII.　　　JUNEAU, ALASKA, MONDAY, APRIL 22, 1895.　　　NUMBER 1.

MURDER MOST FOUL

Attempt made by "Black Jack" Timmins.

AN EDITOR THE VICTIM

Frank E. Howard of the Mining Record Shot Down in Cold Blood.

The citizens of Juneau who happened to be in the neighborhood of Seward and Second streets last Tuesday afternoon about half past five o'clock were startled by hearing three pistol shots fired in rapid succession and almost immediately following, the appearance of Jack Timmins coming from the MINING RECORD office bearing a smoking revolver in his hand. It was but a moment until a crowd had collected at the office when it was learned the most deliberate, cold-blooded, fiendish attempt at murder had been committed, and Frank E. Howard lay up on the floor, bathed in blood, pale as death, and with two bullets in his body from Timmins' murderous weapon.

On account of the large amount of job printing that had been done the week just past for the French Dramatic Company. Monday's edition of the MINING RECORD was quite late and it was not until Tuesday afternoon that the last form had gone to press. At five o'clock the edition was off, the last sheet had been printed, and all hands were rushing the city list out. Eugene C. Stahl, who is associated with Mr. Howard in the management of the RECORD during the absence of Mr. Swinehart, had completed the Douglas City and Treadwell mail and while waiting for the ferry boat he stepped across the street to Brown's bar-ber shop to get a bath. Scarcely had he left when Jerry Eicherly, who was on his way home to supper, stopped to get his paper and have a chat of a few moments with his friend Howard, and it was but a moment later when Timmins made his appearance.

Those who are familiar with the interior arrangement of the RECORD office will remember the table immediately to the left of the door as one enters from the street, and also a second table which is used as a job stone farther back in the corner. Upon the first is a small wire stitcher and it was at this machine poor Frank was seated, hemmed in between the two tables when the cowardly assassin entered. On the outer edge of the table was piled some new job stock which had just arrived and which concealed Timmins' hands and the lower part of his body. Mr. Eicherly was standing at the corner of the table engaged in conversation with Frank at the time Timmins opened the door. Upon entering the office he advanced to the table where his helpless victim was at work, keeping his hands at his side concealed, and said:

"Am I indebted to you for that article which appeared in this week's RECORD?"

"I guess you are," replied Mr. Howard.

"Well, what did you put it in for," asked Timmins.

"It is news and it's satisfactory," said Frank unheedful of his and unmindful of his questioner's intent.

"Then you shoulder the responsibility of the article, do you?" said Timmins.

"I do."

A second time Timmins asked the same question and Howard again replied he "shouldered the responsibility" and "I think we are even now," Eicherly in the meantime having stepped a few feet backward, and was leaning against the frame for type cases at the opposite side of the room.

With that Timmins partially turned toward the door and Howard thinking that was all to be said, arose from his chair, being completely thrown off his guard by Timmins' clever ruse. No sooner had he made a step from the position where he had been sitting when Timmins turned like a flash, grabbed Howard's right hand with his left, and with lightning-like rapidity drew a 38-calibre revolver from his breast pocket and began shooting. With rare presence of mind Frank grappled with his assailant, at the same time knocking the revolver downward the instant it was discharged, the ball taking effect in his left groin. Timmins attempted again to place his gun over Frank's heart, but in the struggle it was discharged to the right of his head, the bullet lodging among some shelves on which job stock is kept on the east side of the room. Made desperate by his failure the craven coward quickly thrust his weapon in Frank's face, the muzzle of the gun being barely four inches from Howard's forehead. Weakened by the continued struggle and the loss of blood from the wound in his groin, Frank with one last Herculean effort knocked the pistol aside, but not in time to escape the ball. It entered his head just to the left of his left eye, ploughing its way through the skull to a point back of his ear where it still remains. With a last look at his helpless victim the assassin turned and passed out on the street. Whether it was his natural cowardice or his fear of the frenzied populace who quickly gathered at the scene that was responsible for his subsequent acts is not known, but he nevertheless lost no time in getting to the court house and giving himself up to Deputy Marshal Hale. He carried his still smoking pistol in his hand and but a few steps away from the MINING RECORD office he joined his law partner, Hamilton, who evidently was waiting for him and from whose actions it would appear was fully cognizant of what had just happened. They shook hands warmly and one would have thought they were long lost brothers—judging from their effusiveness. Together they walked up Seward to the corner of Third where they separated, Timmins going to a murderer's cell which he rightly judged was the safest abode for his rotten and worthless carcass.

After the third shot had been fired Frank made one step and then fell prone on his face to the floor, falling directly in front of the stove exclaiming "I did not think he would do it." Eicherly, who had

$\mathcal{F}$rank Howard, a newspaperman, came north to try his luck in the goldfields. At the time of the shooting, he was serving as acting editor of the *Alaska Mining Record* in the absence of editor and manager, C.B. Swinehart.

Jack Timmins, editor of *The Searchlight*, a rival paper attempted to murder Howard. Timmins was known as "Black Jack " or " Roaring Jack." The latter name he received from the roaring, bull-like voice he affected when drunk, delighted in inspiring terror by chewing bar glasses and spitting the pieces out or by smashing furniture. Quick to draw his Colt's six gun in an argument, he backed most people down. But not everyone. In a card game, he went for his pistol, but found himself staring into the muzzle of the dealer's hand gun. As the story goes, Timmins begged for his life.

In the editorial, Howard commented on Timmins' drunken behavior at the Cohen Brewery fire. According to the editorial, upon hearing the fire bell, Timmins climbed to the top of the building. Setting astride the peak of the roof, he bellowed orders to the volunteer firemen.

"Some people," Howard began his column," are inflated with the idea they are born to command... and often places them before the public in the light of self-conceited asses." The editor continued,"...ringing of the fire bell...aroused Timmins from a stupid state of inebriation...."

Clutching a copy of the newspaper, Timmins walked into the *Record's* office, confronting Howard. When the latter turned away, Timmins shot him twice.

Previous to his attempted murder of Frank Howard, Timmins had been in several shooting scraps. He killed at least two men. In another dispute over a card game, he shot and wounded William Henning. For reasons not clear, Timmins escaped prosecution for that shooting.

The *Alaska Mining Record* for April 22, 1895 carried the story of the attack on Frank Howard.

SIX GUN CENSORSHIP

The citizens of Juneau who happened to be in the neighborhood of Seward and Second streets last Tuesday afternoon about half past five o'clock were startled by hearing three pistol shots fired in rapid succession and almost immediately following the appearance of Jack Timmins coming from the *Mining Record* office bearing a smoking revolver in his hand. It was but a moment until a crowd had collected at the office when it was learned the most deliberate, cold blooded, fiendish attempt at murder had been committed, and Frank E. Howard lay upon the floor, bathed in blood, pale as death, and with two bullets in his body from Timmins' murderous weapon.

On account of the large amount of job printing that had been done the week just past for the French Dramatic Company, Monday's edition of the *Mining Record* was quite late and it was not until Tuesday afternoon that the last form had gone to press. At five o'clock the edition was off, the last sheet had been printed, and all hands were rushing the city list out. Eugene C. Stahl, who is associated with Mr. Howard in the management of the *Record* during the absence of Mr. Swinehart, had completed the Douglas City and Treadwell mail and while waiting for the ferry boat he stepped across the street to Brown's barber shop to get a bath. Scarcely had he left when Jerry Eicherly, who was on his way home to supper, stopped to get his paper and have a chat of a few moments with his friend Howard, and it was but a moment later when Timmins made his appearance.

Those who are familiar with the arrangement of the *Record* office will remember the table immediately to the left of the door as one enters from the street, and also a second table which is used as a job stone farther back in the corner. Upon the first is a small wire stitcher and it was at this machine poor Frank was seated, hemmed in between the two tables when the cowardly assassin entered. On the outer edge of the table was piled some new job stock which had just arrived and which concealed Timmins' hands and the lower part of his body. Mr. Eicherly was standing at the corner of the table engaged in conversation with Frank at the time Timmins opened the door. Upon entering the office he advanced to the table where his helpless victim was at work, keeping his hands at his side concealed, and said:

"Am I indebted to you for that article which appeared in this week's *Record*?"

"I guess you are," replied Mr. Howard.

"Well, what did you put it in for," asked Timmins.

"It's news and it's satisfactory," answered Frank unheedful and unmindful of his questioner's intent.

"Then you shoulder the responsibility of the article, do you?" said Timmins.

"I do."

A second time Timmins asked the same question and Howard again replied he "shouldered the responsibility" and "I think we are even now."

Eicherly in the meantime having stepped a few feet backward, was leaning against the frame for type cases at the opposite side of the room.

With that Timmins partially turned toward the door and Howard thinking that was all to be said, arose from his chair, being completely thrown off his guard by Timmins' clever ruse. No sooner had he made a step from the position where he had been sitting when Timmins turned like a flash, grabbed Howard's right hand with his left, and with lightning-like rapidity drew a 38-calibre revolver from his breast pocket and began shooting. With rare presence of mind Frank grappled with his assailant, at the same time knocking the revolver downward the instant it was discharged, the ball taking effect in his left groin.

Timmins attempted again to place his gun over Frank's heart, but in the struggle it was discharged to the right of his ear, the bullet lodging among some shelves on which job stock is kept on the east side of the room. Made desperate by his failure the craven coward quickly thrust his weapon in Frank's face, the muscle of the gun being barely four inches from Howard's forehead. Weakened by the continued struggle and the loss of blood from the wound in his groin, Frank with one last Herculean effort knocked the pistol aside, but not in time to escape the ball. It entered his head just to the left of his left eye, ploughing its way through the skull to a point back of his ear where it still remains.

With a last look at his helpless victim the assassin turned and passed out on the street. Whether it was his natural cowardice or his fear of the frenzied populace who quickly gathered at the scene that was responsible for his subsequent acts is not known, but he nevertheless lost no time in getting to the court house and giving himself up to Deputy Marshal Hale. He carried his still smoking pistol in his hand and but a few steps away from the *Mining Record* office he joined his law partner, Hamilton, who evidently was waiting for him and from whose actions it would appear was fully cognizant of what had just happened. They shook hands warmly and one would have thought they were long lost brothers judging from their effusiveness. Together they walked up Seward to the corner of Third where they separated, Timmins going to a murder's cell which he rightly judged was the safest abode for his rotten and worthless carcass.

After the third shot had been fired Frank made one step and then fell prone on his face to the floor, falling directly in front of the stove exclaiming, "I did not think he would do it." Eicherly, who had been stricken speechless by the tragedy, turned Frank over on his back, and then summoned John Mein, who was across the street in Miller's butcher shop. Messengers were dispatched for a doctor, and Mr. Stahl, Clarke, Miller, J.C. Howard, the wounded man's father, and Dr. Leonhardt soon arrived.

Kind hands helped Frank to the bedroom adjoining the printing office, and after a hasty examination was made and the flow of blood stopped, it was decided to take him at once to the hospital where the best treatment could be given. A stretcher was procured and hundreds of hands were ready to assist in carrying their friend to St. Ann's. The crowd on Second street in front of the *Record* office had become so dense it was with difficulty that those bearing the stretcher made their way through it.

On all sides were seen the faces of brave, honest, determined men, whose looks were grave and ominous and boded no good for the miserable wretch who had so nearly snuffed out the life of him who thousands were proud to call their friend. Everyone pressed forward to the stretcher to catch a glimpse of the face so familiar to all, and when the death like pallor of it was seen more than one eye was dimmed by an honest ear and ominous looks gave place to distinct curses of righteous indignation, which but a mere breeze would have fanned into an unquenchable flame of vengeance.

At the hospital the wounded man was tenderly carried to room six there, with the assistance of E. Valentine, J. C. Howard and G.A. Carpenter, Dr. Leonhardt finally dressed and bandaged his wounds. An effort was made to locate the ball in the groin, but it could not be reached by the probe. Subsequent developments have proven almost conclusively the diagnosis of the attending physician to have been correct, as it is known the ball did not strike the bladder nor the small intestines. It struck the pelvis bone at an angle which diverged its course downward where it probably entered the muscles of his left leg.

The shot in his head which at first was thought to be of less consequence has turned out to be the more serious of the two. The evening of the shooting a small probe was used in his wound which after entering about two and a half inches struck a hard substance, thought to be the bullet. The following morning, however, after the patient was placed under an anaesthetic a larger probe was introduced and what was taken to be the bullet proved to be a piece of shattered bone. When the probe was removed a small piece of the brain about the size of a wheat kernel was found adhering to the end of it, and it was not considered advisable to carry the search any further. The ball evidently found its way inside and to the rear of the skull, but its precise location cannot be determined. Thursday Mr. Howard suffered intense pain from the wound in his head and the gravest fears were entertained not only by his friends, but the attending physicians as well. Later on the pain decreased and at this writing he is resting as well as could be expected under the circumstances.

While his future condition is purely problematical there is no particular danger apprehended for a few days. Should the ball in his head work into the brain or should a blood clot form there the result of pressure, death would undoubtedly ensue despite the best medical attendance in the world. An operation to remove this shot will not be attempted to only as a last resort on account of the great danger attending it. Of the ball in the groin the greatest fear is that peritonitis may appear, in which event the case would become much more complicated, but would not necessarily prove fatal.

Frank has in his favor an unusually robust constitution, is in perfect health, and above all is cheerful, which is half the battle with grim death. That his rapid and ultimate recovery is most devoutly hoped for goes without saying. He is too valuable a man to this community, too honorable, to brave, too upright and too fearless to be cut down in the prime of life by an assassin's bullet, and those of us who will never forget the prayers taught us by the mother who gave us birth will with uplifted eyes most earnestly implore Him on high to spare the life of our friend and brother.

It is feared he may be permanently disfigured by the powder burns arising from the last shot which was fired at such close range. Quite a number of the grains of powder entered the eye, while around that organ the skin is perforated like a sieve.

Doctor W.G. Cassels was called as consulting physician, and everything in the way of skilled attendance and careful treatment is being done for the wounded man.

AFTERWARD: After the shooting, the *Mining Record* of April 22, 1895 denounced Timmins: "The editor of this sheet has been mercilessly shot down without a shadow of a chance been shown to protect himself from this damnable cur. This same fiend has been a curse to Juneau since he first set foot on Alaskan soil, has been directly or indirectly concerned in nearly every shooting scrap.... Better for him, infinitely better for him, and a thousand times better for the country had he played the solo part in a necktie party.... Better had this miserable body hung between heaven and earth... until the ravens and crows had picked his fetid flesh to shreds." In June 1895, the court sentenced Jack Timmins to six years in the penitentiary. His reign of terror was over.

Frank Howard recovered from his wounds. A day after the shooting, he arose from his bed and insisted on getting dressed.

After the shooting affair, Frank, along with his brother and father, went into the Klondike. Later Frank served as commissioner in several interior towns. Frank Howard lived until 1930, dying in Tanana Crossing, Alaska.

Jack Timmins served time in the penitentiary. Pardoned during the gold rush, he took his wife and young son to the Klondike. Eventually, he moved to Los Angeles, dying there in the early 1920s.

The cross marks the location of the ambush of George Fox and William Mehan by Indians on the McClintock River, Yukon Territory. The map was published in *The Chicago Record's Book for Gold Seekers in 1897.*

40

$\mathcal{I}$n the spring of 1898, William Mehan and George Fox sledded their outfit up the McClintock River, Yukon Territory. At the inlet, the partners camped near a party of Indians. As a gesture of friendship, they gave the Indians tobacco as was the custom.

The prospectors planned to portage over to the Hootalinqua River and pan the sand bars. But, an early warm spell melted the snow, rendering the sled useless. With frontier resourcefulness, the partners cut trees, whipsawed the logs into planks, and began construction of a boat. At some point they had trouble with the Indians.

One account said the prospectors got in an argument with the Indians over "Potlatch." The Indians demanded more tobacco and provisions. Mehan and Fox refused. Suspicious of the Indians intent, the white men broke camp and launched the boat as soon as it was completed. As they pushed off from shore, a deadly rifle fire erupted from ambush.

The *Alaska Mining Record* for September 14, 1898 carried the story of the first legal hanging in the Yukon.

TREACHERY ON THE MCCLINTOCK

Three Indians will be hanged in Tagish in a few weeks. They murdered one prospector and would have murdered another but for miraculous circumstances which enabled him to escape. The crime of the Indians was the most unprovoked, and one of the bloodiest in the history of Alaska. The survivor, George Fox, is here now. He tells the particulars of the thrilling tragedy, which was briefly narrated in this paper last summer, a short time after it occurred.

William Mehan and Fox left Juneau last winter. They sledded a fine outfit on the head of the McClintock river, whence they intended to cross a portage to the Hootalinqua River and work sand bars on that stream. McClintock River empties into the lower end of Lake Marsh, flowing from a northeasterly direction. It is the outlet of a small lake. But when the two men got to the head of the river it was along about the end of May, the portage was bare of snow and they could not sled their stuff over. As the easiest way out of the trap, they set about whipsawing lumber and building a boat to carry them back down the McClintock and up the Hootalinqua. The latter river is the outlet of Lake Teslin into the Lewis river.

Near their camp was a small Indian camp. The white man had "potlatched iktas" (tobacco and other things) with the Indians and had otherwise been friendly to them. When they were leaving camp with their stuff packed in the boat for down-river, Fox took out his watch to note the time. He told Mehan that it was just 10:40.

He had hardly dropped his watch back into his pocket and picked up his paddle when they were fired on by the Indians from ambush in the rear. Fox sat in the bow. He was struck in the back. He fell partly over the side with one arm paralyzed and hanging in the water. He exclaimed: "I'm done for, Bill; pull for your life." But poor Bill did not pull. He was dead--riddled by the bullets in his back, one through the heart.

Fox could not see him but his position enabled him to see the Indians running from the woods down to the shore. Fox moved involuntarily and they let him have another volley, as he lay helpless and bleeding in the boat. One bullet had gone clear through his lungs. But by this time the boat had drifted into rougher water and the second volley struck low. It found lodgment in a sack of flour and a case of corned beef.

The current here set across the river against a point

about half a mile below. The Indians ran back into the woods. The moment Fox saw them run he knew what they intended to do. They would catch the boat as it grounded against the point. It would be all up with him then, if he wasn't as good as dead anyhow. His paddle lay balanced on the gunwale, with just enough of it inside to keep it from falling into the water. He tried to paddle back to shore with his uninjured right arm, but was too weak.

Then another idea struck him. To remain in the boat and be caught at the point was certain death as the Indians would certainly kill him, having begun the job in order to secure their outfit, the watch and their guns; on shore there was a chance for escape. In this critical emergency he placed the paddle into the water perpendicularly to the boat and feebly weaved her around toward shore. Chance favored him, for in a few moments the boat grounded on a small spot of sand near a grassy spit. There was a rotten log lying with one end near the water and the other up the bank.

"I realized at once," said Fox, "the importance of leaving no trail, and for all I could do I feared at least a few drops of blood would escape from my clothes and stain the grass. My clothes were soaked with it. I stepped from grass tuft to tuft as well as I could, for I was rapidly becoming weaker. When I stepped on the end of the log it was so rotten that it broke away. But that was the only mark I left.

"I knew when the Indians got the boat and found only one man in it, they would start back to look for me. So I saw it would not do to stay down near the river, and I made for the foothills. I headed for the mouth of the river where white men were camped and building boats, and there was also a police camp. It took me seven hours to make those ten miles. It was the toughest time I ever had in my life.

"I was so weak that I gave up several times, but after having stopped a few minutes I would set out with

43

renewed determination. I thought I would never get out. Green and yellow lights flashed before my eyes. I was blind and butted my face against trees. My legs would not move. But I said to myself:

"Brace up, old man; don't lie down and die like a dog; don't lie down and die--don't lie down--don't lie down."

"And I kept saying this over and over to myself. I grasped the branches of bushes and trees and pulled myself along, saying first to one leg, "come along here old boy," and then to the other, "come along here, old boy, don't go back on me now." This I shoved, and pushed and pulled myself along through the foot hill brush and bramble.

"God! how I did want a drink of water. My tongue was cracking for it. Little rivulets were right before me but I would not reach them. I felt that if I ever got down on the ground I would never be able to rise again. Once I tried it at what I thought was a favorable brook. But as I stooped over there was an awful pressure on my head behind--the weight of weakness. I barely caught myself in time and straightened up. It is a thousand times worse to see cool water rippling before one's lips without being able to sip it, than it is to be cracked with thirst and no water in sight. Well, I finally got down the river some miles to a white man's camp."

The police started right back up the river. They found the boat well grounded on the point but no Indians were in sight. It seems that the oldest Indian, a man about 21 years old, had been taken sick when the four reached the point. He picked up Mehan's bag and came back to camp with the load. Not finding but one body in the boat, the other three as anticipated by Fox started back up the river to find him or traces of what had become of him. The murdering Indians were divided in opinion as to whether Fox had fallen into the river or escaped. They found the broken log, they admitted afterward and knew he had got ashore and was alive.

The young Indian who had pleaded sick was in his tepee. He had two wives, a young one and an old one. He denied having seen a boat or even a white man in the vicinity. The handcuffs were put on him and he was taken down the river.

The officers started on a hunt for the other natives, but they returned to camp soon after the police left, and learning from the women that the oldest man had been bagged, they took to the woods instantly. The police engaged the services of another Indian and eventually all three were captured farther back in the mountains making for the Cassiar.

They had to depend on their guns for food and were thus tracked. The hired Indian went into their camp pretending friendship. He seized their guns at night and all were soon helpless in handcuffs and lariats. The youngest is only fifteen years old. The Indian captured with the two women was taken before Fox as he lay in bed. Fox had been propped up into a sitting posture.

The Indian's eyes bulged out as soon as he saw Fox, as though he were suddenly confronted by an apparition. He swayed first to one side, then other. He thought Fox had been killed and that he saw his ghost. He threw up both hands and exclaimed:

"Klach!" which, translated, means that he never saw Fox before.

Fox identified all four of the natives at the trial in Dawson. The youngest one was recommended to mercy and will be imprisoned. The other three have been brought back to Tagish, near the scene of their crime, to be executed.

The hanging will take place Nov. 1st next--three at once from the same gibbet. They are young renegades who captured the women and undertook the massacre in order to have a supply of grub to last them through the winter. The coming hanging is already having the desired moral effect on the Indians on the coast and interior. They are all talking about it, and there will be hundreds of them in attendance. Possibly there may be trouble, but it is not thought probable. It is expected to have enough police present to put down any outbreak. Fox will be there.

Mehan was a hard working prospector but he never had much luck. He sold his only piece of property in Juneau to banker B.M. Behrends last winter and started out with a stake.

Fox says he believes that something supernatural helped him out of that boat and pushed him along through the foot hills when he was about to give up, and that the shade of old Bill Mehan will be present at the triple hanging. Had he not been able to escape, almost as a miracle, the natives would have destroyed the boat by fire, obliterated all other marks of identification and their fate would probably never have been know.

AFTERWARD: Fox was taken to Tagish Post where his wounds were dressed. A detachment of the Royal Northwest Mounted Police under the command of Corporal Radd trailed the murderers for two weeks. Unable to escape, the Indians surrendered.

Judge McGuire of Dawson heard their case and sentenced Frank, Dawson, Jim and Joe Nantuck to hang November 1, 1898. The sentence of Frank Nantuck was later commuted to life imprisonment, but he died in jail, as did Joe Nantuck.

The execution was rescheduled to August 4, 1899. Edward Henderson, sentenced for murdering his partner, would also go to the gallows on that date.

Shortly before 8 a.m. three prisoners walked to the gallows. Henderson, a cripple, led the way, helped by the guards. A chair had been placed on the platform for him, but he declined it. Jim Nantuck, cool and in control, climbed the stairs. Contemptuously, he looked at Dawson who crying and moaning had slumped against the railing. Weak with fear, he had to be helped up the stairs.

After a brief prayer by a clergyman, and at 8 a.m.

sharp, Captain Harper nodded to the hangman and the trap was sprung. Fifteen minutes later, Doctors Thompson and Hardman pronounced the men dead. The Yukon had carried out its first legal hanging.

Unidentified members of Soapy Smith's gang
Skagway, Alaska, circa 1898

$\mathcal{J}$efferson Randolf, alias "Soapy" Smith, followed the mining camps, cheating the people with various schemes. One of his favorites was the soap con. Sticking a five dollar bill inside the wrapping of a bar of soap, he offered it for a dollar. A confederate in the crowd bought the bar and triumphantly displayed the bill. Slipping other bills inside the soap wrappers, he sold the bars to the eager crowd. By using slight-of-hand and a detracting spiel, Smith switched the money-loaded bars to plain soap bars. The buyers ended up paying a dollar for a five cent bar of soap. From this scam, he was called " Soapy" and the name stuck.

Soapy hit his stride in Skagway. The gold rush town with its fluid population was made to order for a man of Soapy's talents. He brought to Skagway a collection of frontier toughs, con men, and hoodlums. His men worked the White Pass and the Chilkoot Pass, separating the unwary from their money with various schemes.

In Skagway Soapy operated a saloon and gambling hall. In the backyard, he kept an eagle. When a "mark" went out to see the eagle, he was robbed of his poke. Another scheme was to send telegrams home for the gold rushers. No telegraph line connected Skagway with the outside world, but that did not deter Soapy. He set up an authentic looking "telegraph office," charging various rates and even receiving replies for which he collected fees.

On July 10, 1898, time ran out for the Soapy. In a shoot-out on the dock, between Frank Reid and Jeff Smith, the latter died instantly. Reid fell to the ground with a 45 slug in his groin.

Smith had tried to bluff the wrong man. Reid was

not to be cowed. The Skagway *Daily Alaskan* for August 3, 1898 referred to an earlier shooting where Frank Reid defended himself. At the time, Reid taught school in Sweet Home, Oregon in 1879. A man named James Simmons had, on several occasions, threatened to kill Reid. When he came at Reid with a club, Reid shot and killed him. The jury found he acted in self defense.

The *Alaskan* carried the story of the Smith-Reid shoot-out in the July 11, 1898 edition.

SOAPY SMITH'S LAST BLUFF

The best days work that was ever done for Skagway, was done yesterday evening by City Engineer F. H. Reid, when he shot and instantly killed Soapy Smith. But Frank Reid made an awful sacrifice, for he lies now at the point of death with a rifle ball through his abdomen that may prove fatal.

It was about nine o'clock in the evening when the shooting took place. Smith, who was well under the influence of liquor and worked up to a frenzy, left his house on 6th avenue with a forty-five calibre Winchester over his arm. He went almost on a run down State street, until he came to the wharf, where Reid was on guard. The men had some words earlier in the day, and as soon as Reid saw Smith coming, he knew somebody would get hurt. Smith ran up to Reid and began swearing at him; he then struck at him with his rifle. Reid grabbed at the barrel of the gun with one hand, and drew his revolver with the other. But Smith jerked the rifle away, struck Reid once with it, cutting his arm, and as he raised the gun again Reid pulled the trigger of his pistol, but the cap snapped. Before he could pull again, Smith raised the barrel of the rifle and fired. Again Reid grabbed the barrel and at the same time shot twice in succession. Either ball would have killed Smith instantly.

There were two shots fired into Smith. One shot hit him in the thigh, and the other went into the right side

SOAPY SMITH

of the chest, crossing the body at the left, and going through the heart.

Smith fell dead before the smoke had cleared away and Reid at the same time fell. A crowd, which had followed Smith, closed in on the men. As soon as they found that Reid was alive, some ran for a stretcher, and soon a dozen willing men were carrying him toward his house two blocks away. Before they arrived there, Drs. Moore, Cornellus, and Bryant were on the scene and it was decided to take him at once to the hospital. The men took him up again, and got as far as 5th avenue, when it was decided that the hospital was too far away. Some one ran down the street to make a place ready in a hotel, and Mr. Brogan gladly placed the Occidental at the disposal of the messenger, and told the doctors to take the house.

FRANK REID

Mr. Reid was carried upstairs to a room and in a few moments the physician had his clothes off and found that the bullet had entered the lower right abdomen, and came out at the lower end of the back bone. They immediately began to stimulate the sufferer, who was in very great pain, and to give him morphia.

The trouble that ended in the shooting affray began yesterday at about noon. J.D.Stewart, one of the returned Klondikers, was rolled and robbed of a sack containing about $3,000 in nuggets and dust. Mr. Stewart says that he had gone into Smith's place looking for a companion. He walked out in the back yard, with the bag swung on his shoulder, and was looking at the eagle.

He found out there three men, who from the description given of them afterwards, are supposed to have been Joe Bowers, and old man named Tripp, and another man called Dick. The three men began to play monte, Mr. Stewart says, and finally began to scuffle. He took no part whatever in the game. In a moment or two he found them brushing up against him, and before he knew it, two the men grabbed him, and the third snatched the bag from him and ran. The two men still held him until the third had got well away. Then they too ran in a different direction. Tripp is said to have been the one who got the bag. Stewart's story is corroborated by two reputable witnesses;who saw the whole proceedings from adjoining building.

The alarm was raised at once and the marshal was notified. Marshal Taylor told those who gave the alarm that if they would keep quiet for a time he would get the men and the money, but in a few minutes the marshal started up Broadway with a carpenter to oversee some work he was doing, and the men felt that he was not very much interested in the case. In an hour the whole town was alarmed and excited.

Judge Sehlbrede was telephoned for, and he promised to come over from Dyea as soon as he could get a boat. He telephoned back asking that every precaution be taken to allay any agitation, so that he could be free to act when he came.

Consequently the newspaper men got together and decided that the best interests of the town would be best served by their remaining silent on the matter until Judge Sehlbrede could act.

Between 2 o'clock, when Judge Sehlbrede was sent for, and 6 o'clock when he arrived, at least a dozen men went to Soapy Smith and tried to get him to disavow the robbery and give up the men. But to every appeal he said that no one had been robbed, that the man had entered a gambling game and had lost his money fairly. So he declined to do anything about the matter, finally making the excuse that if Stewart had not "hollered" he would feel like going out and getting him a piece of the money.

Judge Sehlbrede sent for Smith as soon as he got in town. At 5 o'clock Smith went to the marshal's office where the Judge was. They talked the whole matter over in the presence of Marshal Taylor and a representative of the *Daily Alaskan,* but to every appeal Smith made the same answer--the boys who had the money won it in a fair game and they should keep it.

He also said he had a hundred men who would stand behind him and see that they were protected. The judge finally told him he could not afford to stand up for a gang of thieves, but he almost screamed--"well, Judge, declare me in with the thieves. I'll stay with them," and with that he passionately beat the table with his fist and left the room.

Again Judge Sehlbrede sent for him, an hour later, and talked with him. But it was always the same. He would do nothing and "would stand by the boys." He did offer to give up one of the men, but he made his surrender conditional upon certain men being appointed to guard him.

Judge Sehlbrede declined to submit to any conditions and he called upon those who were with him to know whether, if he issued warrants, they would arrest Smith and his whole gang. The Judge was told that every man of them would be brought in. He said he wanted the men. If he issued the warrants, alive if possible, but dead if necessary. And this plan was in preparation when Smith was seen running down State street to his death with a rifle on his shoulder.

Along about the middle of the afternoon while perhaps twenty men were standing on the corner of Broadway and Fifth avenue discussing the affair, Smith passed through the crowd. Some one used his name and suggested something about his being such a coward that he had to have a gang of men with him. He heard the remark and turned around on the crowd, with an oath, threatening to litter the street with corpses. No one defied him, but from that moment Smith's days in Skagway were numbered by the citizens in that crowd. They knew that Smith had to be killed, driven out or presented with a quit claim deed to the town. That he himself thought something of the same thing is shown by his exclamation to Denny Brogan, who was trying to argue with him; "Well, I am about due to kill a man and I have lived long enough myself anyway."

Inside half an hour from the time the shooting took place, two hundred citizens were organized into a company. Judge Sehlbrede appointed Captain Tanner special officer and Tanner at once organized his men. He had every house suspected of harboring one of the Smith gang raided and search, and guards were put on every wharf along the bay on the hillsides, and the railroad people were notified of the occurrence, set guards along the north of the city and on the bridge with a view to round up the remnant of the gang.

At 1 o'clock this morning Frank Reid was taken to the Union hospital and at 5 o'clock Dr. Whiting, the railroad surgeon, who had been sent for the night before, operated to locate the course of the bullet, and the damage done by the wound. Dr. Whiting afterward came down town and said that he believed that the intestines and bladder were not hurt, but that the abdominal cavity was perforated and a peritonitis might ensue, which would be fatal. The pelvis or hip bone was shattered and he took out a dozen pieces of splintered bone. Dr. Whiting thinks that though Reid is a very badly injured man he has a chance to recover, though he must under the most favorable conditions, take a long time to get well.

After Reid had been attended to Judge Sehlbrede went down to the wharf to view Smith's body. He placed a guard of five men over it, and ordered them to remove it to the undertaking establishment, which was done. Judge Sehlbrede held an inquest today.

The town after the shooting last night was nearly wild. All sorts of rumors were afloat and more shootings, lynchings and the like were talked about, but presently Captain Tanner showed so conclusively that he was the proper man for the leadership of the men that quiet prevailed and every one felt that the worst was over.

AFTERWARD: Soapy's gang tried to hide from the posse, but determined men armed with Winchesters routed the gang members from their hiding places. Some came in voluntarily. Dan Tripp hid out in the woods until Sunday when hunger drove him out. Captured in the Pack Train restaurant, "... gorging himself on a beef steak and mushrooms," he remarked, " I would rather be hung on a full stomach than die of starvation in the d--- mountains."

The posse discovered several of Smith's men hiding in the cemetery. Ordered to come out, with their hands up, some one after a brief pause, shouted "all right." Bowers then stepped from cover with his hands up, followed by Winters, alias " Slim Jim," and Wilder. When the prisoners were marched into town, a mob gathered, some carrying ropes. Armed men confronted the posse, demanding the prisoners.

Commissioner Sehlbrede faced the angry crowd. Appealing to their sense of right, he convinced them to let the law run its course. He then ordered the prisoners to be removed to the second floor of the Burkhard Hotel. A short time later, Slim Jim jumped from a back window and tried to escape. Recaptured by an angry mob, he begged for his life.

The committee questioned anyone suspected of being involved with Smith. The July 11, 1898 edition of *The Alaskan* listed 27 men arrested by the vigilantes. The posse escorted 10 aboard the ship, *Tatar* and told never to return, others were tried by the court and sent to prison.

On July 20, 1898, Reid died and he lies in the Skagway cemetery, not far from where Jefferson Randolf Smith is buried. On Reid's tombstone is carved the words: "He gave his life for the honor of Skagway."

LAYING ON THE LASH

Hanson was flogged at Sheep Camp on February 11, 1898 for stealing supplies. He received twenty-six lashes. *The Skaguay News*, February 18, described the whipping: "The cords swung into the air and then fell like lightning on Hanson's back. Swifter and more furious they came, each stroke bringing out in bold relief, great welts from which the blood began to trickle slowly at first and then faster, until the man's back looked like a huge piece of raw flesh…"

SHEEP CAMP

Located thirteen miles from Dyea, Sheep Camp sprawled along a wooded valley. At the height of the rush, the camp had a population of about 1,500 people, living in tents, log cabins and shacks. Sheep Camp was four miles from the Chilkook Pass and the last major camp before Lake Lindeman. Today only a few rock building foundations remain of the once bustling settlement.

While packing over the White Pass and Chilkoot trails, the gold rushers left piles of unguarded supplies and equipment. This was too much of a temptation for two thieves, William Wellington and his partner, Edward Hanson. They stole cached goods on the White Pass and carried them over to the Chilkoot to sell.

The owner of the supplies trailed the thieves to Sheep Camp on the Chilkoot Trail and identified his goods. Miners formed a court in the Big Tent Saloon and tried the thieves and administered frontier justice. The court cut the telephone wires between the camp and Dyea to prevent anyone from interfering with the punishment

Newspaper man Stroller White printed the story in *Stroller's Weekly,* November 20, 1930.

SHEEP CAMP VIGILANTES

While the rush was at its height, thousands of tons of goods of all descriptions were piled in hundreds of caches, and, quite unguarded, formed an irresistible bait for those dishonestly inclined.

Skagway, the beginning of the White Pass Trail, was the headquarters of these gentry, and two of them formed the idea of stealing the whole outfit of a man who was one of the comparatively few who were playing a lone hand and going in by themselves. He had moved his stuff a mile or two up the trail, and had returned to Skagway on some business which kept him there for several days. The two thieves seized the opportunity, took everything back to town, and loading it into a rowboat, freighted it to Dyea, the starting point of the old Chilkoot Trail, the real "Trail of '98."

The two thieves landed their loot on the beach at

Dyea, joined the throng of mushers on the trail, and as they thought, were lost in the crowd. But Nemesis in the shape of their victim was on their heels. He kept in the background and allowed them to get as far as what was known as Sheep Camp with all his belongings.

On account of Sheep Camp being the last good camping ground with firewood before the summit was crossed, there was quite a congestion at this point, and a mushroom town sprang up. Enterprising individuals built cabin roadhouses; others opened little stores in tents, and there was even a bar in what looked like a small-sized circus tent, called the Big Tent Saloon.

Upon reaching Sheep Camp the owner of the stolen goods decided to start something. He found, after interviewing a number of the campers that stealing from the caches was rapidly increasing and the majority of them had suffered more or less from the depredations of thieves and were ripe for some action to put an end to both the robbers and their activities if necessary.

An impromptu meeting was immediately held by those who had been approached by the Skagway victim, and it was decided that a beginning should be made with his case.

After some discussion a committee of five was appointed, who appointed one of their number as chairman. His name was Martin, a very capable man. Several of the crowd were then chosen by the committee to act as policemen, with instruction to immediately arrest the two accused, or rather three; for on arriving at Dyea the two robbers had taken an innocent old Englishman in with them as partner.

A number of notices written by hand were then posted at conspicuous points along the trail to the summit saying that a meeting would be held at the Big Tent Saloon the evening of the next day. The date was on or about February 15, 1898--to take measures for putting an end to the stealing on the trail. The three men were under arrest, confined in a log cabin close to the Big Tent

Saloon

The next evening the Big Tent Saloon was filled to overflowing. The stock and fixtures had been taken outside. The chairman and committee who constituted the court were seated on a board resting on two boxes. A table made of rough lumber with a box on it for a seat was placed in the middle of the tent. On this the accused were seated in full view of all the tent, and the rest of us who, I suppose, could be termed the jury, were closely packed five or six deep around the sides. The tent was lit by a number of ordinary coal oil lanterns and candles.

The accused had been kept separate from one another, and given no opportunity to concoct a story as to how they had become possessed of the outfit; and of their doings previous to coming on the trail.

First one would be brought in and questioned; he would then be taken outside and his story checked up by that of the next one. This was repeated several times, and it became quite plain that--with the exception of the old Englishman they were lying wholeheartedly.

It began to look very black for them when the proceedings were brought to a sudden and dramatic finish by one of the accused, who gave his name as Wellington. He had just been taken out by a guard, and the other a stocky and stolid young Swede named Hanson, brought in, when a shot was heard close to the tent. Immediately afterwards a man rushed into it and yelled, "Wellington has shot the guard and has run down the trail." There was a sudden hush for a few seconds and then cries of "After him! Shoot him!" and one of the committee had just shouted, "Get a dog team, he can't leave the trail," when a second shot sounded some distance away.

Another silence held the crowd motionless and speechless for a minute or two, broken by a voice outside the tent saying, "It's all right boys, Wellington has shot himself and is lying in the trail now." This precipitated an immediate rush for the trail.

The crowd found the body of Wellington lying in

the trail about 100 yards from the tent. By the light of the lanterns it was a ghastly sight. He had fired a shot from a heavy .45 revolver into the middle of his forehead, and his face, powder-blackened and mutilated, was unrecognizable.

There was some dispute as to whether it was Wellington or someone who had grappled with him in his dash for liberty and been shot down, particularly as he was without the canvas coat he had been wearing, until someone pointing out that a rather unusual blue cloth cap he wore was still on the back of his head.

"This is Wellington, right enough," a grim-looking individual remarked, followed by, "Well, he is settled; now let's go back and hang Hanson."

"Yes, we'll hang Hanson," roared the crowd and rushed back to the tent.

But the suicide of Wellington changed the mood of the crowd and it was decided to whip Hanson instead of hanging him.

The young Swede was taken to an open space on the trail at noon the next day, most of the mushers coming down from the summit to witness the sentence carried out. He was made to strip to the waist. It was about 10 below with a wind blowing and he had four flannel shirts on.

The prisoner was taken to a tall stump about a foot in diameter standing in the center of the clear space, and his wrists tied together with his arms encircling the stump. A flogging was administered.

The first few cuts with the rope the culprit endured stolidly, but soon began to squirm, attempting to climb the stump and cried, "Why don't you hang me, this is worse than hanging." The more tenderhearted in the crowd then commenced to shout "Enough! that will do, turn him loose"! countered by "Give it to him, he's a thief, lay it on" from the sterner and more revengeful ones.

One of the storekeepers shouting "Yes, he's a thief," was suddenly confronted by an angry looking individual who, eyeing him disdainfully, said, "You're as much a thief as he is, you damned cheat." But the storekeeper was dead game and retorted with, "Don't call me a thief, you're another!" or words to that effect. After glaring at each other for a second or two they simultaneously drew their shooting irons and it was curious to see the crowd as the guns appeared, instinctively draw back out of the line of fire, leaving a clear lane behind each one of them. However, a quick-witted individual jumped in between them saying, "That will do, none of that now." And they were separated without any damage being done.

The accused was given a number of cuts with a rope end to his bare back and then sent down the trail with a stern warning never to show his face on the Chilkoot again.

From that time until the stampede was over there was absolutely no more stealing on the trail. At any rate on that part of it which ran through the disputed territory. The evil-doers and thieves were given an example and a warning which sank in. They realized that the decent ones were not to be trifled with and would protect themselves.

AFTERWARD: The vigilante court held at Sheep Camp was the last of its kind. When Dyea authorities heard of the punishment meted out at Sheep Camp, they sent a message for the men involved to turn themselves in. The vigilantes responded; "Come and get us." No one ever did.

$\mathcal{B}$ ands of primitive Indians roamed northern British Columbia, Yukon and the Northwest Territories as late as the 1940s. Witchcraft was a common belief among these bands. This belief led to acts of violence against tribal members suspected of sorcery.

In 1924, a boy was killed by a band of Liard River Indians for being a witch. The Northwest Mounted Police were asked to investigate the murder by British Columbia officials. At that time, no roads penetrated that northern wilderness. To interview witnesses and to make an arrest, the Mounties traveled nearly a thousand miles by canoe and on foot. Inspector Sandys-Wunsch and Constables H. W. Neville and C. R. Martin arrested five Cree Indians for murder and took them to Vancouver for trial.

The story of the witchcraft murder appeared in *The Wrangell Sentinel*, October 2, 1924.

THE WITCHCRAFT MURDER

Officers of the Canadian Royal Mounted Police arrived in Wrangell Sunday afternoon on the *Hazel B* with five Indians whom they are taking to Vancouver to await trial on the charge of murder. The five prisoners are in charge of Inspector T.V. Sandys-Wunsch, and two constables of the Royal Canadian Mounted Police.

Because he was believed to be a witch, a seventeen year old Indian lad, Atolar Moccasin, had his hands tied behind him and was hung up head downward and left to freeze to death, when the temperature was below zero. Later he was taken down and buried, and it is believed that he was buried alive.

Mining men arriving here on the same boat with the prisoners state that Frank Bass, store keeper in charge of the Hudson's Bay trading post at Liard, reported to government authorities that Big Aleck, a Cree Indian from the McKenzie River, had told him of the murder of an Indian boy charged with witchcraft by nomad Indians from the Nelson River while the later were camped forty miles below the Liard post.

Superintendent R. S. Knight of the Royal Canadian Mounted Police sent out a patrol to investigate. Inspector Sandys-Wunsch and Constables Neville and Martin arrived in Wrangell early in June and took the river boat to Telegraph Creek. The trip into the wilderness where the murder was reported was one of hardship and was reached after traveling hundreds of miles on foot with pack dogs and navigating the swift waters of the upper Liard in a canoe.

Big Aleck became apprehensive when he was finally located by the officers and flatly denied that a boy had been killed in that vicinity. The officers remained camped near the Indians, notwithstanding their evident hostility. A few days after their arrival one of the Indians fired at Captain Sandys-Wunsch. The Captain did not return the fire although he holds the world's record for revolver shooting and could easily have dropped the fleeing Indian.

The officers remained in the vicinity of the Indians for two weeks in their efforts to get a clue. One day they came upon a hole which had been scratched out by wolves down to some heavy old planks. The officers made a larger opening, and upon removing the planks found the body of a boy with his hands tied behind him.

One of the Indians happened along as the body was being dug out and was terrified, believing that another witch had told the officers where the body was buried. The Indian also believed that he heard the dead boy speak to the mounted police who had dug him up. After that it was easy to get a confession from the Indians.

The confession was that Edie, a woman, had tied the boy Moccasin up head downward to drive the evil spirits away because Big Aleck had a dream that the boy was a witch. A girl named Lucy came along and found the boy before he was dead and wanted him cut down. The Indians claim that they cut him down before he was dead but killed him by hitting him on the head with a rock before burying him.

Inspector Sandys-Wunsch also holds a commission as a magistrate. He arrested Edie and her three brothers, Dan, Jimmy, and Clem, and also Big Aleck, and took them to Liard for a preliminary hearing. The hearing brought out further facts, and the Inspector decided to take the prisoners to Vancouver to await trial in a court of competent jurisdiction.

The prisoners talk a little English but are primeval in appearance. They all wear moccasins and the men are fitted out in overalls and cheap coats from the trading post. The woman has a two year old child with her. Two other small children were left behind.

On this trip the prisoners are having their first contact with civilization. The steward on the Stikine River boat said they ate ravenously of meat, but regarded the bread that was offered them with suspicion. On their way from the boat to the jail they stared at the three story Wrangell Hotel building in wonderment, and when they saw Jack Gurr riding a bicycle they all stopped and stared at it in amazement.

A small child playing near the customs house was holding a cat in its arms when the prisoners passed through the court house lawn. This not only attracted their attention but aroused their deepest interest. They had probably never before seen a domesticated animal other than a dog.

On entering the U.S. Marshal's office a guard pressed a button which lighted the room. They were plainly frightened at this sudden flash of light, and stood gazing at it while waiting to be taken into the jail proper where other mysteries awaited them in the form of a bath tub and running water.

The prisoners frequently laugh when talking to each other, and apparently have no consciousness of guilt or apprehension as to what will happen to them when they are brought before the big white chief at Vancouver. Captain Sandys-Wunsch and two constables will remain in Wrangell until October 6 when they will leave with the prisoners for Vancouver on the *Princess Alice*.

AFTERWARD: Tried in Prince Rupert on August 20, 1925, the court convicted Big Aleck of manslaughter in the death of Atolar Moccasin Jim. But, it acquitted Jim, Dan, and Clem Loat. Edie Loat, the Indian woman, was not sentenced at that time.

MINERS OF ALASKA HANG A MURDERER

Cowboy Tanner Swings From a Tree for His Crimes.

Two Men Fall Before Bullets of the Desperado.

Quarreling at a Tent Leads to the Slaying of Friends.

DARKNESS SAVES SOME LIVES.

Trial Follows Fast on the Tragedy and Thirty-Nine Prospectors Conduct the Execution.

[Special Dispatch to "The Examiner."]

SEATTLE (Wash.), February 2.—With the arrival of the Pacific Steam Whaling Company's vessel Alliance, Captain Hardwick, from the Copper river district this afternoon came news of an atrocious double murder, done at Valdes, Prince William Sound, January 24, and the subsequent hanging of the assassin.

The men whose lives were taken for little or no provocation were N. A. Call of Worthington, Minn., and William A. Lee of Lowell, Mass. Milter Filmore Tanner, a Montana cowboy, was their slayer. He was executed the following morning. Forty-four men said that he should die, and as thirty-nine of the number preferred the rope route as the best means of disposing of the murderer, he was accordingly hanged.

During the fall rush to the Copper river section there came to Seattle a Massachusetts expedition. Here the members of this crowd found Tanner, who, though without money, sought to get into Alaska. These men outfitted Tanner and made him one of their party.

Arriving at Valdes the expedition went into winter quarters. Tanner, Lee, Call, Haines and Pearce occupied the same tent. It came to a question of providing better shelter. Tanner, it appears, quarreled with

his tent mates about the work, making himself so disagreeable that the other four occupants held a consultation in the tent, deciding that the cowboy should be given his share of the outfit and told to search for quarters elsewhere.

While this conference was going on Tanner stood outside and near the tent eavesdropping. He heard nothing good of himself. The words that came to his ears set him in a rage. Going to a neighboring tent, where he had left the weapon, he secured his revolver. He returned, and, pulling back the tenting which hung over the entrance, he informed the quartet inside that he had heard what they had said about him. Call spoke, saying:

"Look here, Tanner, if you can't act as a man you will have to get out."

"You can't," replied the cowboy, "after bringing me to Alaska, make a fool of me."

With this he drew his revolver and fired, killing Call, who was seated. A second shot dropped Lee to the earth and a third bullet put out the light, an incident which saved the lives of Pearce and Haines. Lee expired within ten minutes. Both were shot through the right lung.

Tanner remained at the threshold of the tent waiting, as he subsequently declared, for Haines and Pearce to come out that he might kill them also.

They, however, remained inside, and meanwhile a man named Scott came upon the murderous Montanan, who coolly announced that he had killed two of the occupants of the tent and was waiting to put the other two out of the way. Scott gave the alarm, and a young man named Miller of Buffalo, N. Y., unarmed, walked up to the bloodthirsty cowboy and demanded his revolver. Tanner surrendered it willingly.

That night the forty-four residents of the camp accorded him a trial. King, a San Francisco attorney, presided as Judge. The trial lasted from 10 p. m. until 4 o'clock the next morning, and the accused was found guilty. He was defended by one of the Massachusetts expedition. A question arose as to the method of procedure after conviction. A vote was taken, and thirty-nine favored hanging, two or three shooting and one or two wanted the murderer sent to Sitka for trial. The rope men, being largely in the majority, had their way. Tanner was hanged from a tree limb at 10 o'clock the morning of January 3d. Just before being strung up he was asked:

"Boys, are you aware that you are hanging the best shot in Alaska?"

His last words were: "Boys, are you going to jerk me up and down or pull me up straight?" and when informed that it would be a long and straight pull he added: "All right, boys; let her go."

A. C. Labbe of San Francisco, who witnessed the execution, said he never saw such an exhibition of nerve. Tanner declined to make a statement, other than to say that at nine years of age he was left an orphan. Call and Lee were men of families. Their bodies, as also that of Tanner, were buried at Valdes.

The San Francisco Examiner
February 3, 1898

$\mathcal{V}$ aldez claimed the first hanging in Alaska, but that rather dubious honor goes to Juneau. There, in the early 1880s, a group of miners hanged two Indians for the murder of a whiskey peddler and a jail guard.

The Copper City hanging had its genesis in Seattle in 1897. An eastern party of prospectors bound for Alaska met a Montana cowboy named "Doc" Tanner in Seattle. Impressed by the cowboy's tales of the frontier, the group invited him to join the expedition--a fatal mistake.

According to the *Seattle Daily Times* issue of January 3,1898, "Doc" Tanner became overbearing and arrogant. When the party reached Cooper City [later called Valdez], the original organizers met in one of the tents and decided Tanner and his bullying ways had to be dealt with. The group planned to divide the goods, give the cowboy his share, and send him on his way.

Unknown to the men, Tanner had overheard them. Returning to his tent, he retrieved his revolver, and confronted them, saying: "I overheard your talk about me and I'm here for business." Shooting twice he killed Call and Lee. During the confusion, the candle was knocked over, plunging the tent in darkness. Dropping to the floor, the other two men escaped through the back of the tent.

.   The miners surrounded Tanner and he surrendered without a struggle. He commented: "I had intended to get them all." An unidentified and undated clipping from a Valdez paper quoted Tanner's last words as: "Well Boys, I want to know how you are going to hang me. Pump me up and down or hang me straight?"

"We'll do the best job we can with our limited experience," one of his captors responded.

The *All Alaska Review* printed a detailed version

The cross indicates where the rope was thrown across

The Examiner [San Francisco] carried the above sketch of the hanging tree and A.C. Labbe in its February 8, 1898 edition.

A.C. Labbe was an eye witness and a participant in the hanging of "Doc" Tanner. Ironically, the miners hanged Tanner with his own rope. Labbe wrote: "Tanner's rope was properly prepared for the occasion with soap so it would run easy...Twenty-four of us pulled on the rope and the execution was over... buried Tanner at the foot of the tree on which he was hanged."

of the hanging in the May 1915 edition.

HANG ME STRAIGHT

"Gentlemen, you're hangin' the best man with a six-shooter that ever came to Alaska or any other country. I want only one shot to a man. All right, boys; fire at it."

These were the last words of Doc Tanner, the first man hanged in Alaska, before be was hoisted to eternity by a rope that hung over the limb of a tree near Valdez on the morning of New Year's day, 1898.

Winfield Scott Amy, the builder of the first cabin in the place where the city of Valdez now stands, and one of the discoverers of the great Bonanza copper mine, told the story of the hanging to the *All Alaska Review*. He was one of the jury, was the man who arrested Tanner and was present at the last awful moment. This is Amy's story:

"A party of seven men, from Massachusetts, who came to the district near Valdez in 1897, met Tanner in Seattle. He looked like the real thing for Alaska and they asked him how he would like to go North. He agreed, but stated that he had only about $300 which he wanted to blow in first. They decided to buy an outfit for him and they all went North.

"When they arrived near Valdez and looked over the outfit Tanner declared the amount of provisions not sufficient for the sum of money spent and he asked to see the receipts. An argument ensued and there were indications of a split-up. The partners assured Tanner that they would make it all right, but he seemed to harbor the belief that they were going to throw him out.

"On the evening of the last day of the year 1898 three of the party, Call, Stinchfield and Dunn, were in their tent when Tanner entered. He declared he wanted 'things straightened out,' and they again assure him that such would be done, but he went out and returned in the evening with a revolver. The three men sat on boxes which the light of a candle threw their shadows like ghosts over the canvas. At the first shot Call fell dead. The second shot killed Stinchfield. But this shot also put out the light, and Dunn threw himself forward on his stomach, so avoiding a fate similar to that of his companions. Indeed, Dunn was the man whom Tanner chiefly wished to get, and he thought he had succeeded.

"Randall, another member of the party, traveled down on snow shoes the distance of two miles to our camp and related to us the story of the shooting. Stevens and myself went up. We found Tanner. He still had his gun and, although we were unarmed, we took it from him. I have that gun still in my possession. When I asked him for the gun he said:

"'All right, Amy, but don't let those fellows get at me when I'm unarmed.'

" The trial took place that night in the cabin which Tanner's party was building. In the district at the time were forty-five men. Five refused to act, and one of the remaining forty was selected as judge,while the remaining thirty-nine acted as jurymen.

"The trial lasted from 11 o'clock that night until 4 o'clock next morning. Then we found a verdict of guilty, and Tanner was sentenced to die that morning.

"We sat around the cabin until daylight. Tanner was the coolest and calmest man I ever saw. I have seen three men hanged by bands of citizens, but this man was the coolest. He seemed to be absolutely careless and never showed the slightest sign that he troubled in the least about his approaching doom. His face was without the least expression of fear.

"At daybreak we broke a trail with snowshoes to a tree some distance away from the cabin, and at 9:30 a.m., we brought him under the limb which was to be his gallows. Just at 10 o'clock we told him we were ready."

"'All right,' he said, quietly.

"Dunn, who had so narrowly escaped death at

70

Tanner's hands, had made the request that he be allowed to put the rope around the doomed man's neck, and we granted him the privilege, but he was so completely unnerved that he was unable to place the rope and could not have done so if he was trying yet. Others had to help. We had tied his hands and feet and as he stood on the threshold of eternity he appeared still to be absolutely without the the least care as he looked at us. Then we asked him if he wished to leave any word for his relatives."

"'I have no relatives,' he said.

"When asked to state what he wanted done with his clothes he requested that they be given to one of our party named Reed."

"' Don't want your clothes,' said Reed. 'I wouldn't wear them.'

"We then asked him as to the disposal of his part of the outfit and he requested us to sell it and give the money to the families of Stinchfield and Call. When we asked him if he had anything else to say he answered in the same quiet undisturbed manner:

"' No, gentlemen; you're hanging the best man with a six-shooter that ever came to Alaska or any other country. I want only one shot to a man. All right, boys: fire at it.'

"Death came quickly and the body was left hanging while the bodies of Tanner's two victims were being interred. Later the body of the murderer was also laid to rest, and two years afterward those who took part in the hanging received official notification from Washington that they were exonerated from all blame.

"To this day no one knows who Tanner was, except that he was probably a cowboy from Montana."

AFTERWARD: Little is known of Millard Fillmore "Doc" Tanner. From Lexington, Kentucky, he probably drifted west to Montana as a young man. Before he died on the gallows, he commented: " I had to rustle from the time I was 12 years old; and I have no one to give [my] things to."

The other two men in the tent at the time of the shooting, Pierce and Haines, crawled through the back of the tent and escaped. This story has an ironic twist. As an incentive to Tanner to join the group, Call gave his pistol to the cowboy--the revolver Tanner later used to kill him and Lee.

Tanner was hung from a tree two miles east of Copper City, later known as "Hangtown" and finally Valdez.

No further details of the surviving members are known. If the party followed through with their original plans, they packed over the Valdez Glacier Trail into the Copper River country. Some newspapers and steamship companies touted this as the "All American Route," the easiest way into the goldfields. In reality, the Valdez Trail was a nightmare of glaciers, mountains and rapids. One newspaper editorialized that the Chilkoot Trail was a boulevard compared to the Valdez Trail and the rapids on the Yukon were dry when matched against the ones on the Valdez route.

$\mathcal{W}$alter Pierce recorded the first hanging in Juneau City. Two Indians were found guilty by a miners court of killing a whiskey peddler and a jail guard. The murders followed the peddler's refusal to give whiskey to the Indians.

This account has a twist of irony in it. Pierce participated in the miners court that condemned the Indians to death. A few years later he was charged with the murder of an Indian and the wounding of another man in a similar argument involving whiskey.

At the time, Pierce managed the Music Hall--a saloon-dance hall-- in Newtown, a settlement across the channel from Juneau. Newtown, a collection of saloons, cabins, shacks and mine buildings, was a typical frontier settlement with all the vices. Miners frequented the Hall to drink and dance with the Indian women.

Near midnight on Saturday, October 16, 1886, several drunken Indians entered the saloon, demanding whiskey. Pierce ejected them from the Hall. In retaliation, the Indians smashed windows. Apparently, a general fight broke out with Pierce receiving cuts to his face. At some point in the fight [The Sitka paper called it a riot] two shots were fired, killing a Kake Indian named Klu-Kleetz and wounding a white man, Frank Mchrwalt in the chest. Both of the men were innocent bystanders.

Pierce was taken to Sitka and tried for murder. At the trial Pierce's lawyer argued his client did not fire the shots that killed Klu-Kleetz. Witnesses said the shots came from outside the Music Hall. Another witness for the defense testified that Pierce was bleeding so profusely from cuts on his face that he could not see to shoot. Found not guilty, Pierce returned to Juneau.

Walter Pierce recorded Juneau's first hanging in

his book, *Thirteen Years of Travel and Exploration in Alaska*, published in 1890 by Journal Publishing Company, Lawrence, Kansas. But, he did not mention the saloon fight and the resultant murder charges against himself.

JUDGE LYNCH'S COURT

"Unfortunately among the white population, there were some unprincipled scoundrels who made it a business to sell vile whiskey to Indians. As there were no laws forbidding the sale, we had made our own mining laws and a clause to that effect. Yet there were some who paid no attention to this, and on several occasions it became necessary for the miners to seize and destroy their poisonous mixtures.

"One of this class of men located himself on a trail leading from Juneau back to the portion of the district called the basin. This trail was largely traveled by Indians. The reprobate had built a log cabin where he was doing a rushing business selling whiskey.

"One evening three Indians came along who were intoxicated before they came to his place. They had no money, but demanded liquor: He refused them credit--a fight was the result and the white man was killed. One of the Natives struck him on the head with a club and broke his skull. The Indian who did the deed was one of the most lawless of his tribe, and there were strong suspicions that he had killed white men before. The next day after committing the murder, he asserted that he would kill more white men yet.

"Now the Indians had been very saucy and impudent all summer. There being a great many more Indians than white men, they had received the impression the whites were afraid of them. So a citizens meeting was called, and it was decided that it would not do to let the murder go unnoticed. It was thought best to arrest him and turn him over to the United States authorities at

Sitka.

"As we knew that the gunboat would be over from Sitka in a few days, the arrest was made at once. He resisted and was aided by the two who were with him when the murder was committed. This made it necessary to arrest the three. A man was appointed to guard them and they were locked up in a building that had two rooms. The guard occupied the front room and the prisoners were locked up in the back room. They were confined there about one week, when one of the prisoners, pretending that he wanted to do some sewing, asked and received permission from the guard to sit in the front room, as the back room was too dark, there being no window.

"The guard was armed, but foolishly and carelessly had allowed his pistol to lie on the table in the room. This was what the murderous, treacherous Indian wanted, and watching when the guard turned away for an instant, he seized the pistol and shot him in the back. Then unbarring the door released the other two, and all three ran off to the Indian town, taking the pistol with them.

"The Indian town is situated about one half mile from Juneau, and the time when this occurred there were at least one thousand Indians in the village. The murderous act was partly witnessed by a miner who was near the building. He foolishly, alone and unarmed, followed the three fugitives who ran into an Indian house. He attempted to enter also, when the Indian who had the pistol shot him dead at the door.

"At once all was excitement, both in the Indian and in the white settlements, and a conflict appeared to be inevitable. The miners were notified in every direction and all came to town. Fortunately we had plenty of arms and ammunition. The Indians far exceeded us in number, for we could not raise more than two hundred and fifty men, while the Indians could raise a thousand. Yet we had the advantage of being well armed, while they had nothing but old style shot guns. Still it was our desire to avoid a conflict, as we could not profitably fight Indians and mine at the same time. For in case of a continued war much property would be exposed to their depredations, and also many isolated parties of miners who were out prospecting, might be killed.

"Yet it was necessary to punish the murderers, as it would not do to let them commit such murders and go free. A small detachment of armed men was sent to the Indians to demand the prisoners. We found the Indians all armed, but they did not appear to wish to fight. We called for their chiefs, who came forth, and we spoke to them, telling them that we must have the prisoners; that we did not wish to fight with and kill others of them who were innocent of crime; that we only wanted those who had murdered our friends; that we wished to remain on friendly terms with them; that if they did not give them up quietly we should be obliged to take them by force, and that we would be assisted by the government, who would send gunboats to help us.

"This had the desired effect. After considerable talk amongst themselves they agreed to give them up. The chief pointed out the house they were in and told us to go and get them, that they would not interfere.

"We found the door barred, and they would not answer when we asked them to open. Procuring a large stick we quickly battered down the door and entered. They had got a board loose on the back side of the hut, and, jumping through, attempted to escape. But escape was impossible, as the house was surrounded.

"The Indian who committed the first murder, still having the murdered guard's pistol with one load in it, placed the muzzle to his temple and blew out his brains, thus cheating the gallows. We secured the other two and took them back to Juneau, passing through almost the entire length of the Indian village. On our return we passed by groups of natives. They had put away their arms, but looked sulky and threatening.

"A meeting of all the citizens was at once called, and consultations had as to what should be done with the prisoners. It was decided to at once appoint a judge, impanel a jury and give them as fair a trial as possible in the absence of proper authority and law. This was done. All witnesses were examined, the evidence was positive and very strong. The verdict of the jury was: 'Guilty of murder in the first degree.' The sentence was death.

"A committee was at once appointed to build a scaffold. It was built on the beach in plain view of the Indian village, in order it might be a lesson to them. All things being completed, the prisoners were brought forth under a strong guard.

"It may be said to their credit that they showed no signs of fear. They both made short speeches in which they expressed themselves willing to die, and they had confidence that they were going to a happier land. They advised their friends to live at peace with the white man and conform to his laws; also to avoid the use of whiskey and other intoxicants. They said that they forgave their enemies and asked all to forgive them. Having spoken thus they pronounced themselves ready.

"The black cap was put on, the noose adjusted, the trap sprung. When they had hung long enough, their bodies were cut down and taken away by their relatives. This ended the unfortunate affair, but it had an excellent effect on the natives afterwards. They were quite civil to the whites, and although this occurred several years ago, there has never been any trouble with them since."

AFTERWARD: Walter H. Pierce remained in Juneau until June 1889. Broken in health by the privations he suffered on the northern frontier, and living in poverty, Pierce expressed a desire to return to the States. His friends raised money for him and he left on the steamship *Ancon*. Locating in Denver, Colorado, he ran a cigar and fruit store.

" ... we witnessed a sight that made our blood run cold. A thousand hideously painted savages were rushing a poor woman toward the beach. The crowd gathered around her dancing and chanting. ...in half an hour, when the crowd dispersed, only the bones of the woman were left. Every particle of her had been eaten by cannibals. We dare not fire a shot or enter a protest, so poorly were we fortified, and so greatly were we outnumbered. [1857]

William Duncan, missionary
Fort Simpson, B. C., Canada

Cannibalism was a common practice among some tribes of Alaskan and Canadian natives. Hudson Bay Company traders and missionaries reported acts of murder, and the consumption of the victim's body. Father William Duncan, a Presbyterian missionary, witnessed a cannibalistic ritual at Fort Simpson, British Columbia in the 1850s.

The strangest story of cannibalism to come out of the North Country was the account of W.H. Pierce, early prospector and explorer. He recorded a deadly encounter with cannibals in his book, *Thirteen Years of Travel and Exploration in Alaska*, published in 1890.

THE MAN EATERS

"Years before I had been told by a Russian trader, who had been trading on the Yukon, about a tribe of cannibals that lived on the head waters of the Tananah, a river tributary to the Yukon. I knew that the Tananah River was still several hundred miles further westward. Little did we think that we were camped within five miles of those horrible man eaters. Being at the lowest point we intended to go to, we wanted to stop here several days before starting back.

"All unsuspicious of danger, we were out prospecting every day. Sometimes we went up small streams, and having mining tools to carry, we did not take any arms with us. Foolish, careless men. It cost us the lives of two of our best men, who were murdered and eaten by those horrible inhuman wretches.

"These two men had started in the morning to go to a place where they had been sinking a hole, and having found a small prospect they wanted to try to sink to bed rock. They took nothing with them but their tools and a lunch for their dinner. All came to camp in the evening except those two men. The place where they were prospecting was down the river and a little way back from it, making it three miles from our camp and directly back about three miles from the camp of the man eaters.

"The next day we commenced searching for them, but without success. We found Indian tracks, and also discovered the Indian camp. No Indians had visited our camp which satisfied me that they meant mischief. They surely knew that we were there, as we had fired guns at geese and ducks the first day we landed, and fired, more or less every day afterwards.

"We were now on our guard. Those who had camped across the river moved to us. All our arms were put in order and ammunition got ready. Fortunately, all were well armed with repeating rifles--principally Winchester--with two exceptions, and they were breech loading shot guns which were good with buck-shot at close range. There were also the arms belonging to the two missing men.

"No one had been to where the men were prospecting, but we knew the direction they had taken. So in the next day's hunt we found the place. There was no evidence of a struggle there. We hunted all day and found nothing more. Their tools were there and the case was a puzzle. We were now thirty strong. That evening we discussed the matter. We could not think of moving away and leaving the men. It was decided that the following day ten men should, if possible, try to follow the men's trail; that ten should go to the Indian camp on pretence of wanting to trade; that five should stay in camp; that five should go in a direction immediately between the Indian camp and the place where the men had been prospecting; that in case there was any firing, the middle five should at once reinforce the party where the firing was, and that all should then get back to the camp, where we would be governed by circumstances.

"We thought it might be that they had made

prisoners of our two comrades. I became one of the party who went to their village. We were well armed and determined in purpose. We walked boldly down the river and without warning walked suddenly into the village. At first it created a great excitement among them. Some disappeared, others more bold, stood their ground. Having been requested by the other members of my party to act as spokesman, I at once laid down a cloth or piece of calico that we had brought along for the purpose. I placed thereon numerous small articles, such as Indians trade for. This they understood, and at once gathered around in great numbers. I had instructed my men to watch their every movement, and also not to allow them to crowd too closely. I made a line on the sand which indicated to them I did not want them to cross.

"They brought forth furs and skins of kinds, and began to trade. I was not deceived in their appearance. They were extremely large and powerful race, a few of them being less than six feet height, and the women were almost as tall as the men. The weather was warm and they wore but little clothing. Some of them did not wear any, being entirely naked. Others wore a skin covering or breech cloth, fastened at the waist, and hanging down almost to the knees. Their hair, which is very black and straight, hung loose down to their shoulders. It was matted and full of vermin. They were extremely dirty. I do not think they had ever washed themselves.

"Their features were more like those of wild beasts than those of human beings. Their eyes were of the Mongolian type. Their foreheads were low and receding. In some cases the chin would be receding, in others the reverse. Some of them had heads of unusual length behind, almost amounting to a deformity. All had the wild beast expression of countenance, and showed a lack of intelligence. I have seen a good many wild tribes but have never seen before, and never expect to again, a race of human beings which could give one such feelings of loathing and disgust as these Alaska man-eaters.

"Their language consisted of a succession of harsh and unpleasant sounds connected with signs, and I had concluded that they had little or no dealing with traders; as I could not see any articles in the camp which they could have traded for, excepting some old knives and a couple of very old axes. Their arms were bows, arrows and spears. From some source they had got iron that formed their spear heads, although some of them were made of copper. Their arrows were pointed with bone, and some carried clubs with rocks fastened to the end.

"I finished trading as quickly as possible, as I wanted to go through the village, to see if I could see any thing pointing to the fate of our missing companions. Their houses were made of sticks, brush, grass and the skins of moose and caribou. We walked boldly through the village, and inspected every thing that came in our way, but found nothing.

"We then went back of the village into the timber. We saw numerous trails which appeared to lead farther into the timber. I also noticed that there was a great deal of fallen timber close behind the village. I afterwards found I had done a good thing in posting myself so well.

"We then returned to camp, and had not been there long before the other two parties came in. They had found some evidences of a struggle not far from and farther down the little stream where the boys had been prospecting, but had found no trail leading from the spot. Some of the party wanted to leave, claiming that we could do nothing more. To this I would not consent, and the majority sided with me.

"There was much difference of opinion as to what was the best course to pursue. We decided that the next day a party should go again to the place where the struggle had been and search farther. That night two of our men had gone a short distance from camp in the evening, and were returning late, saw some of the natives sneaking around our camp, but had not been seen themselves.

"This satisfied me that they were guilty of murdering our companions. I also believed that if we attempted to leave without punishing them they would attack us. The country being rough and full of underbrush, they could kill a great many if not all of us. However, I did not say any thing then, but next morning joined the searching party. We left about one half the men in camp, the remainder making the searching party.

"We went to where the struggle had been. The evidence of a struggle was quite plain, and in the creek close by, we found a button. Evidently it had been torn off there. This satisfied us that they had walked in the water to avoid making any trail. We followed down, and about one mile below found the place where they had climbed out on the bank. There was a great number of tracks, most of them coming from the direction of the cannibals' village.

" From then on the trail was easily followed. It led us about five miles to a small stream, that ran through a small open glade. Here the horrible tale was told. Several fires had been built, and in the bushes at the edge of the glade, we found the bones of our unfortunate companions. We could see that they had been roasted, and some of them plainly showed the marks of teeth.

"At once it flashed across my mind that we should keep the man-eaters ignorant of our discovery. I spoke to the others about it. They at once coincided with me. So we did not disturb any thing, but turning toward camp went back as soon as possible.

"Then the question arose, what should be done? A few wanted to leave at once, and I am glad to say only a few. They were the bar-room fighters of whom I have previously spoken. I let them talk and said nothing, although most of the men had been looking to me for an opinion. At length several asked me to express my opinion, which I then did.

"I told them it was self-evident that the man-eaters were not afraid of us. Had they been afraid, they would have left at once after committing the horrible act. That I believed they were only waiting until we should begin to travel, when they could destroy us with their arrows from ambush without exposing themselves. That I believed they were watching us continually, and since I had carefully reflected on the matter, I believed our caution about the discovery was useless.

They then asked me what I thought they should do. My proposition was to attack them in their village and kill as many as possible and teach them to respect the whites. We could then return in safety. As we were armed with repeating rifles, and they had no idea of our power, they would be so much surprised that the victory would be easy. Whereas, if we started back without punishing them, we would have the same number to fight and also would do it at a great disadvantage. Having talked the matter over, they adopted my plan and war was decided on. The following morning was appointed for the attack. We decided to start at daybreak, go down through the timber, and attack them from the rear.

"The men insisted on my acting as captain of the band, which I consented to do provided all were satisfied, which they were. I then told them that I should expect them to obey promptly any order given by me. To this they consented, and we lay down to rest. I scarcely slept that night, but lay thinking of the possibilities of the coming day. Would we all be alive by the next sunset? I knew that they out numbered us almost twelve to one, but I had great faith in our Winchester; besides, fully one half of the men had Colt's revolvers.

"The nights then were very short, there not being over two hours darkness. As soon as dawn appeared I got up, stirred up the fire and got the men up. We made a large kettle of coffee, of which all partook, some also eating a light breakfast. I told the men I wanted them to be very careful and not expose themselves. I pointed out to them how inconvenient it would be if there were many wounded. Although I was positive that we should carry the day, yet we could do it without exposing ourselves. I said that we should keep behind trees; that if they pressed us too hard we should avoid a hand to hand fight by slowly retreating from tree to tree. That when we had them checked, we should regain the ground by again advancing from tree to tree.

"I advised them to make no move which would effect our position, unless I gave the order. I then appointed a man to act as my assistant, my main object being to prevent the men from needlessly exposing themselves. I left five men in the camp, and with twenty-four went through the timber and came out behind the man-eaters' village.

"It was as I had expected. They had been watching us and there was a great clamor and noise. I could see that they were armed and ready. I formed the men in a line with instructions to keep as near in that position as possible, and keep under cover of the trees. Placing my lieutenant at one end of the line, I myself went to the other. This would enable us to watch and if any were wounded we should see it at once; whereas, if the men were scattered too much, we should not know where to look for them, and in case of retreat we might accidentally leave wounded men in their merciless hands.

"I then ordered the men to advance, keeping themselves covered as they had done. Closer and closer we got, and the noise increased in the village. I then gave the order to fire whenever they had an opportunity to kill anyone, but to fire no useless shots.

"We did not wait long. I saw they were getting ready for a rush toward us. I got upon a fallen tree trunk, but yet managed to keep behind another tree. I saw the natives start and sung out to the men that they were coming and to make every shot count. On they came. The whole horrible, brutish-looking lot came fairly under fire at less than one hundred yards distant. I opened the ball by firing the first shot, and then the rifles rang out on the still morning air; steady and regular. Then I saw what a terrible weapon the Winchester was in the hands of good marksmen. Down they went by scores, almost every shot appearing to count one, and yet they kept coming. Now they were within one hundred feet of us.

"They had come to the fallen timber that I have before spoken of. They were obliged to climb up on it to get to us, which exposed their whole bodies at a very short range. Not one could gain an upright footing upon the timber. When the front one fell the next one tried it, only to fall dead in the arms of his brother cannibals behind. They were checked; they wavered, then broke and ran. They had lost terribly for so short a time. I then ordered the men to advance as far as there were trees to cover their movements. We got so close to their village that we could fire through their frail houses.

"They fired arrows at us, but we were not exposed and they did us no harm. A few of them sneaked up behind some fallen timber and used their bows, but it was all guess work.They also threw some spears over a pile of fallen trees, behind which some of our men were. A spear struck one of our men in the knee, making a severe but not dangerous wound. This was the only man of ours who was hurt during the fight. They had enough of charging us.

"Taking seven men, I passed down to the lower end of the village where I could keep in the timber and still get closer. There we got a splendid chance, firing on them in front as well as in the rear. They were now getting it too warm to stand it any longer. They became panic stricken. Some jumped into the river and swam across; others were shot in the water, and some got away through the unguarded space at the upper end of the village. At last there was nothing more to fire at. Some women and children were hid in the huts, but the most of them had got away. When we discovered their hiding places they screamed and ran. We let them run, paying no further attention to them.

"We had killed one hundred and four, and about

thirty were so badly wounded that they could not get away. Some of our men wanted to kill them, but I objected. I thought we had punished them enough, and I think their appetite for the white man's flesh is spoiled for many years to come. We burned their village and destroyed everything of any value that we could see. We went and got the bones of our murdered companions and buried them, and started on the return trip. We did but little prospecting on the return. All were dejected in spirits. Our provisions were getting short.

"Bad as those wretches were, I can never think of them without feelings of compassion. Their punishment was almost too severe. I did not regret the killing of the men. They had made war on us in the most treacherous manner. But If I had to do it over again I would not have burned their village and their fur clothes and bedding, for that must have caused much suffering among the children in the long, cold winter that followed."

AFTERWARD: Very little is known of Walter H. Pierce. As a young man he came North in the spring of 1877 to the Cassiar gold fields. For the next 12 years he prospected and explored in the Yukon, British Columbia, and Alaska. The privations he suffered on the frontier broke his health. In June of 1889, he left Juneau and went to Denver where he ran a cigar and fruit store. He died of consumption.

SENSATIONAL GUN FIGHT AT NOME

EX-POLICEMAN SHOT AND KILLED

Bitter Feeling Between Chief of Police Jolly and Ex-Police Officer James Causes Trouble.-- The Latter Shot Three Times.-- Died 30 Minutes Later.

By Telephone from A. E. BOYD, Special Correspondent to The News.

A fast, fierce and exciting shooting scrape took place at Nome at 3 o'clock on Friday afternoon last, when Chief of Police John Jolley shot and killed Ex-Police Officer James.

The shooting took place in front of the Warwick saloon. A howling, blinding blizzard prevailed at the time, and few people were on the street. Those who were in the immediate vicinity say that three shots were fired, and a young man who was passing asserts that he heard Jolley say, "You can't do that with me."

The trouble which led up to the shooting arose over the fact that James had been discharged by Jolly from the police force, and a feeling of bitterness was thereby engendered.

Just prior to the shooting James was gambling in the Eldorado saloon. He had been drinking heavily and was in a highly excited and nervous condition; betting five and ten dollars a throw on the crap game. Jolly came into the saloon, and James spoke to him, but Jolly cut the conversation short by walking out of the place. James followed him out, and a few minutes later three shots were heard.

A crowd of people gathered around and Dr. Rininger was sent for, and immediately on his arrival he had James taken to the hospital on a hand sleigh. The doctor picked up a gun beside James. It was cocked, but had not been discharged.

Dr. Rininger stayed with James until he died. In describing the wounds the doctor said that one bullet entered the left hand above the wrist, passed downwards and out through the palm; another bullet entered the head above the right cheek and lodged in his brain, and another passed through his neck. James died at 3.30, precisely thirty minutes after the shooting occured. At no time did he regain consciousness.

Immediately after the shooting Jolly gave himself up at the Federal jail. He was interviewed by the district attorney, after which he was seen by a representative of the Nome News, to whom he made the following statement:

"I discharged James from the police force on January 4, and he gave over his star to me yesterday. I knew that he felt very bitterly towards me and this afternoon he saw me in the Eldorado saloon, and began to talk 'mean.' He had his gun in his overcoat pocket at the time, and I knew him to be a good shot. My gun was in my inside coat pocket, and my overcoat was buttoned up over it. James said to me 'I ought to kill you now.' I left the place to try and get away from him, but he followed me out. I met a friend on the street, and we stopped to talk. Noticing that James was following me, I took advantage of this opportunity to unbutton my overcoat so that I could reach my gun in case of an emergency. I then passed on in the direction of my home, and he kept following me. I turned around and said to him, 'This thing has got to stop.' I saw him draw his hand holding a pistol from his pocket, and I fired. I don't know how many times I fired."

The Inquest.

An inquest on the body of Ex-Police Officer James was held before Commissioner T. Read on Saturday. The jury was made up as follows: Ed. Spencer, W. H. Dohrman, W. J. Rogers, F. H. Thatcher and J. F. Giese. The examination of witnesses was conducted by Assistant District Attorney Grigsby, Attorneys Albert Fink and P. C. Sullivan being present to watch the proceedings on be-

$\mathcal{J}$ohn J. Jolley was born in New York City on January 4, 1845. Little is known of his early history. According to the Montana *Anaconda Standard*, Jolley came to Montana in 1878 and worked as a blacksmith. About 1884, he gave up blacksmithing and located on a ranch near Melrose, Montana. Soon after moving to the ranch, his wife and children died. Their death affected Jolley very deeply. The *Standard* wrote: " a great change came over Jolley immediately after. He appeared to have lost all ambition...."

Selling the ranch, he returned to Butte. Apparently well known and popular, he was elected city marshal in 1886.

About the time he took office, he invested in a saloon on Main Street. After his second term in office, he started drinking heavily and "Bucking the Tiger" at various gaming houses. In the Mint Saloon, an argument erupted into a fight with Billy Blyth, a gambler. In the fracas, Jolley stabbed Blyth in the neck.

It was not a fatal wound and the gambler had nearly recovered from the stab wound, when he caught pneumonia. While delirious, Blyth jumped from the third floor of his room, receiving several compound fractures, severely damaging the arm. The doctor decided to amputate the arm, and Blyth died on the operating table.

For the assault, Jolley was sentenced to three years in Deer Lodge penitentiary. Pardoned by the governor after having served 18 months, Jolley went to Nome in the fall of 1899 where he was hired as Chief of Police.

Apparently, Jolley served the gold rush town for over four years with out incident. But trouble appeared in the form of one of his deputies, Samuel James, and

Lottie Wilson, known in Nome as "Miss Lottie." She charged James with failure to pay her $75.00 he owed her, claiming to be his housekeeper. Additionally, she accused James of stealing city property and coal from the Northern Commercial Company's warehouse.

While investigating the charge, Jolley suspended James. According to Jolley, James starting drinking very heavy and threatened to kill him. At three o'clock in the afternoon in front of the Warwick Saloon, Samuel "Jim" James pulled his "belly gun," a Colt's Derringer, advancing on Jolley and the Chief fired, killing James. Immediately after the shooting he was interviewed by the district attorney. After which he made a statement to the *Nome News*:

"I discharged James from the police force on January 4, and he gave over his star to me yesterday. I knew he felt very bitter toward me, and this afternoon he saw me in the El Dorado saloon and begin to talk mean. He had his gun in his overcoat at the time, and I knew him to be a good shot. My gun was in my inside coat pocket, and my overcoat was buttoned up over it.

" James said to me, 'I ought to kill you now.'

"I left the place to try to get away from him, but he followed me out. I met a friend on the street and we stopped to talk. Noticing that James was following me, I took advantage of the opportunity to unbutton my overcoat so I could reach my gun in case of an emergency. I then pressed on in the direction of my home, and he kept following me. I turned around and said to him: 'This thing has got to stop.' I saw him draw his hand holding a pistol from his pocket, and I fired. I don't know how many times I fired."

Jolley gave the following account during his preliminary hearing. It differs in tone from the first terse account. In this version Jolley portrays himself as being very conciliatory toward James. The story appeared in the *The Nome News* under the date line of January 13, 1903.

THE LAST GUN FIGHTER

The morning of the 4th of this month, January, a messenger boy came to me and said, "There is a woman in No. 6 of the Columbia House wants to see you."

I went up there to see her. I believe they call her Miss Lottie. She told me James owes seventy-five dollars for work done for him.

I said to her, "My dear lady, I cannot help that."

"Well, she said, "I can send him to McNeil's Island, and, I will if he don't pay me this $75."

"What has he done." I asked?

She replied, "He has stolen coal from the N.C. Co. to my personal knowledge. He has stolen pistols. He has stolen coal oil out of the city jail."

I went to James' room immediately and confronted him.

"James, Lottie sent for me this morning and accuses you of stealing. I am going to lay you off, and I am going to investigate this charge that is brought against you."

"She is a d--- liar."

Now, Jim I said, "You have been drinking a good deal lately, you gambled, and I am afraid you have been neglecting your duty as a policeman."

The next time I saw him, I upbraided him for drinking and staying with the woman that put the charges against him. I told him, "Jim, instead of you helping me out or helping yourself you are going to the dogs as fast as you can go. You had better sober up."

And he said, "Jack, I am sober," but he was pretty full then. Then he added, " I don't give a d--- anyway."

On the morning of the 7th, he came to my house a little after 8 o'clock in the morning to see about going back to work on the police force. I told him, "Jim, I can't put you back yet, and if you don't sober up, I will not put you back."

He threatened me: "Jolley, if you don't put me

back, by G--, I will kill you."

He called me a --- --- ---; abused me like a horse thief in my own house. I told him not to use such language, on account of the people that lived next door. I tried to reason with him: "Jim when you get sobered up, you will think better of this, you will think better of me. I wish you would go out now, I don't want you in the house." So he ran his steam out there and he went off after he blew off his talk.

The next time I met him was the evening of the 8th, in front of the Hub saloon. He was standing there, I think it was Finnigan who was with him. Walking up to him, I said, "Good evening, James." He gave me a grunt and reaches me out the star and key. I took the star and key and turned it over to Finnigan. I walked around town for a while, but I did not see him any more that night.

So the next day I came up the street and James was standing in front of the Eldorado saloon, but I did not see him until I got right up close to him. I said, "How do you do, Jim."

He looked at me and replied, "You --- --- , if you ever mention my name again I will kill you, and I have a good notion to do it now."

I asked him, "Jim, what do you want to kill me for? What have I done that you should talk to me like this?"

He said, "If you don't put me back on the police force, I am going to kill you. I am fixed for you." He had his hand in the side pocket of his coat.

Jim, I know you are fixed. I actually thought he would give it to me right there in the street. I told him, "You can't expect me to put you back on and you threatening to kill me this way, and everybody looking on."

We were walking all of this time. I started right off to try to walk away from him. When we got in front of the Old Pioneer saloon, he stepped right behind me and over onto my left. I was trying to get out into the middle of the road. He stepped on my left, and had a Derringer in his pocket all the time. Puts it up to my ribs, and said,

"You old --- ---. I am going to blow your belly out now."

I said, "Jim it won't do you any good to kill me. Haven't I always treated you right? Haven't I always given you money when you came to me and wanted it?"

"He replied, "G--- d---, I am broke and out of a job and don't value my life that much," and with his left hand snapped his finger right in my face. Then I tried to work back again on the sidewalk. I didn't like the road then. I thought he might go into the Hunter saloon. Instead, when I saw he didn't go into Hunter way, I turned to the left and sheared out into the road. Then he whirled in front of me and stopped, and said, " G--- d--- you, I am going to kill you anyway."

I said, "Jim, you must be crazy."

He replied, "Jack there's no use in talking. I will kill you or you will kill me now."

Jim, "I don't want nothing at all to do with you." I didn't say anything to provoke him because I knew he would give it to me the first bad word that I let go.

When I stepped away from Jim to speak to a man who approached me, I faced him so that I would look at Jim. [while talking to the man, Jolley unbuttoned his coat to get to his pistol.] Jim pulled his hand out of his pocket with his Derringer in it. I threw up my hand and warned him. "Jim, you can't come like that on me." He started right for me. He probably took two of three steps toward me. Jim didn't think I was looking at him, but I was watching him all the time. I fired. Then I don't know how many times I fired nor I didn't know whether the man was standing up or laying down, to tell the truth.

After Jolley's testimony, the court heard the testimony of the witness to the shooting. The examination of witnesses was conducted by Assistant District Attorney Grigsby. The defendant's attorneys, Albert Fink and P.C. Sullivan, were present. The first witness called was George Wilkinson, who gave his testimony in a clear, direct manner.

He said, "I was walking along the sidewalk in the neighborhood of the Warwick building, going in a westerly direction, when I heard a shot. I looked and saw James falling. There was another shot and after James was on the ground there was a third shot. Just before the first shot Jolley said, 'Don't come none of that on me, James.' Jolley was about four feet from James. At the second shot James was falling forward and sideways. James was nearer to me than Jolley. Then I ran away. When I came back James was lying on the ground. His hat was off, but I did not see a gun. I did not hear any remark, except what Jolley said."

The first to be called after the noon recess was Albert Wile who testified that he was working in his tailoring establishment near the scene of the shooting, when he heard a shot and rushed out to see another flash and finally the third and last shot. He saw James lying prostrate, and some distance from his right hand a cocked Derringer, which was partially covered by his cap, lay on the ground. Witness then heard Jolley say, "You boys see this cocked gun; there is a man there (indicating) on the sidewalk who saw everything."

James McCoskric testified that he "saw part of it." He was in Dr. Hill's drug store when he heard a shot. He was near the door. As he went through the doorway a second shot was fired. He saw a man in the street standing over a prostrate form and he started to run in that direction. When he reached Hunter way, about 25 feet distant, a third shot was fired.

"When I reached the spot," said the witness, "Jolley was standing about five feet from James' head. I said: "What's this?" And Jolley replied: "He pulled a gun on me and I done him up. There is a man (pointing to the sidewalk) who saw the shooting."

"I told Jolley he had better fetch a physician. I saw a gun beside the man. A hat was partially over it, but I saw that the gun was cocked. A crowd gathered fast. I told them to let the gun alone, as a murder had been committed. James was breathing hard and moaning. I was the first one to speak to Jolley."

Wm. McIntosh took the stand. He is the man that Jolley referred to when he said to McCoskric: "There is a man who saw the shooting." He saw Jolley and James walking along the middle of the street and he hastened to overtake them as he wanted to speak to Jolley about a dog. He stepped from the sidewalk.

McIntosh said, "I spoke to Jolley; he pulled a gun and I run. I did not hear anything said. James was 10 or 12 feet ahead of Jolley. I ran back to the sidewalk. By this time two shots were fired. I saw James fall. He was five or six feet from Jolley, and fell toward Jolley. Jolley was standing east of James.

"When I first saw Jolley and James they were in front of the Hunter saloon, walking side by side. I did not hear any conversation. Was within two or three feet of Jolley when he pulled his gun. Did not notice anything out of the ordinary about him. Did not see anything in James' hand. When I spoke to Jolley, James was about five feet ahead of him."

Charles Chang Eng, the Chinese cook of the N.C. Mess house, was next called, and in very good English gave an accurate description of what he saw, being an eye witness. In his testimony he designated Mr. Jolley as the "fur coat man" and said he saw him and James by the Dexter saloon. Chang Eng was walking on the south side of Front St. and noticed Jolley was preceding James a few feet; Jolley crossed the street and James started after him; then Jolley fired.

He further stated that when James started after Jolley his right hand held a gun, which dropped by his side when he fell from the effects of Jolley's bullets. When asked whether or not he heard Jack Jolley say anything immediately after the shooting, he said, "Him fur coat man," he say, 'the man he had a gun in his hand and I done him up.'"

George Baldwin testified he, George Wilkinson and Ed. Stevens were passing along the street, on the sidewalk on the north side of the street, going in a westerly direction.

"I saw James at the edge of the sidewalk, and heard Jolley say: 'You can't come that on me, James.' James was east of Jolley and facing him. His right side was opposite to me, but his right arm was crooked, as though it were in his overcoat pocket. I could not see his right hand. James lunged forward like a man going to fight. I did not see Jolley until after the first shot was fired. I was watching James. When I saw Jolley he was pointing the revolver toward James and I noticed that one of his fingers--the middle finger--was extended along the barrel. There was a slight pause between shots. At the first shot James started to fall forward, but turned and fell on his back. I saw Jolley put his gun back in his pocket, and then I ran."

AFTERWARD: After the preliminary hearing, Jolley was bound over to the Grand Jury which indicted Jolley for willful murder, and a bail was set at $5,000.

In June, Jolley was tried for by the Federal District Court in Nome. After hearing the arguments and testimony, the jury acquitted John J. Jolley on all charges on June 6, 1903. He probably left Nome before the freeze-up in 1903. His name no longer appeared in *Polk's Directory,* an early day listing of towns and people in Alaska and the Yukon.

ℬorn in the glaciers and mountains, the Nushagak River flows 250 miles out of a wilderness teeming with game and fur bearing animals into Bristol Bay. In the 1920's a man the Indians called Klu-tok, "The man from the Mountain," claimed the headwaters of the Nushagak as his own. He administered death to trespassers. A lone wolf, he hated everyone, Indian or white man. The number of men he killed is unknown as is the reason for his hatred of mankind. His story appeared in the *Cordova Daily Times*, July 3, 1928.

THE MAN FROM THE MOUNTAIN

Aroused over the murderous career of a crazed Indian in the upper Nushagak River district, residents of Dillingham have voiced a plea for aid. For years the Indian had reigned supreme until now the region is absolutely unsafe to travel. It is hoped that some help will be given this section of Alaska to apprehend this crazy man, at whose axe and gun are laid the responsibility for possibly a score of murders near here in recent years.

The man believed responsible for the murders is known as Klu-tok, a full-blooded native Indian born on the Nushagak River, Bristol Bay. He is 35 years old, 5 feet 4 inches tall, and weighs about 135 pounds. The Indians call him "Man from the Mountain." He reigns supreme at the headwaters of the Nushagak River and on a small river called the Tik-Chik.

The Indian is a lone wolf, shunned by and shunning the outside world, neither friend of white man or native. All the other natives in the region fear him, as well as most white man.

97

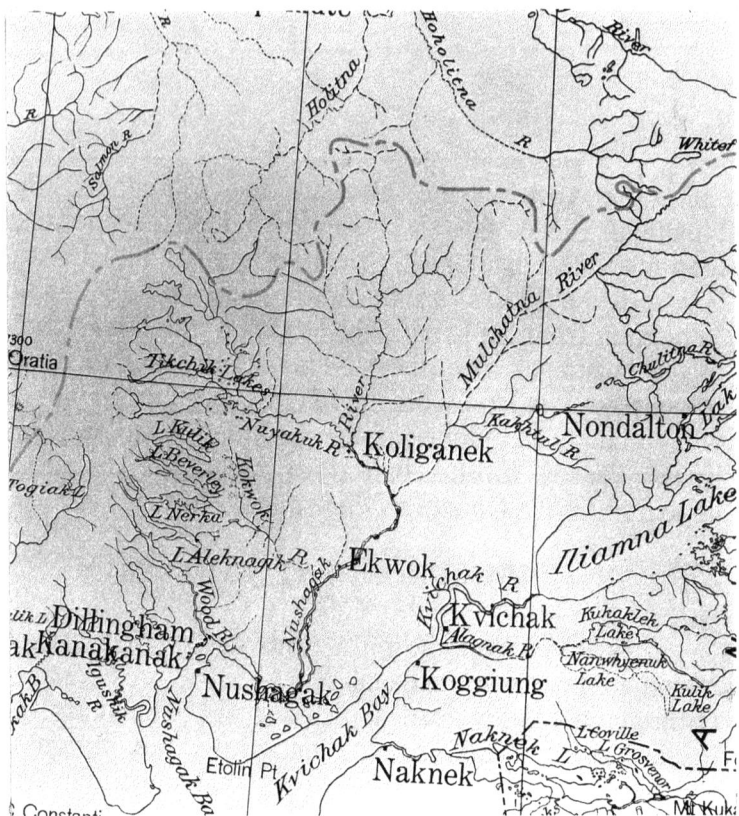

KLU-TOK'S COUNTRY

The Man from the Mountain controlled three hundred and fifty square miles of wilderness lying between Tikchik Lakes, the Mulchatna River and the head waters of the Nushagak River. A throwback to an earlier time, Klu-tok lived off the land, using the survival skills of his ancestors. His only concession to the Twentieth Century was a 30-30 rifle used to hunt man.

Through some system that is unknown to white men, Klu-tok keeps in close and constant communication with what is going on in the surrounding country. By what is termed "moccasin telegraph," he seems to know when any man enters his territory, and he goes after all invaders.

Disdaining to use the weapons of civilization for his own use the half-crazed Indian shoots game with a bow and arrow. He packs a 30-30 rifle for his human prey. To act as his guard when he is asleep, he has a small dog.

Traveling alone, his domain in a kayak or skin boat--apparently always well dressed--the Indian has for the past nine years been carrying on his reign of terror against the encroachment of outsiders.

Klu-tok first became notorious in 1919 when it is said that his career of crime started by killing two natives and at the time he boasted, he "would kill two more all the same as moose."

From that time until the present he has had the whole upper reaches of the entire Nushagak River under his control, keeping trappers and prospectors out or at least on their guard all the time. He leaves arrows in front of his cabin to warn people to keep off his trail.

On April 15, 1927, Harvey Sakrison, an American white man, together with Charles Anderson, an Indian, born on the Nushagak river, went up that river to trap beaver.

They landed about 35 miles from where the Chu-chit-nok River joins the Nushagak at Jack Aho's cabin. They trapped until the 22nd day of May of the same year, having marked off the calendar until that time, then left a note on the table for Jack and Ole Wassentry, and left for their trap line. They had previously made arrangements with Aho and Wassentry to meet them there at the cabin about that date and go down the river together.

On the 25th day of May, Jack Aho and Ole Wassentry came to the cabin, found the note and took the

99

dogs and started back to Sand Point, so as to be on time for the fishing season. They expected Harvey and Charley to follow as soon as they had taken their limit of beaver.

However, time passed on and they did not show up, so on the second day of July the case was reported to the authorities. There was not evidence enough for the officials to act, so the local men took it on themselves to act.

Hutch Smith, a prospector, and Ole Wassentry took their boat and started out to look for the missing men. After traveling 245 miles and searching for several days they found Harvey's body in the river about two miles from Aho's cabin. The body was caught by a sweeper and only the shoulders were visible. Smith and his companion had been instructed that if there was sign of foul play to leave the body where they found it and report to the commissioner.

They secured the body on the shore and left to search for the other missing man. The search was unsuccessful, so they returned and reported their find to the authorities. The commissioner authorized a body of five men to go up and bring the body down. This was done, and after the body was taken from the river, one man took it down, while the remaining four continued the search for the partner of the dead man. They continued their search for five days and then gave up in despair. They reported to the commissioner and the case was dropped for the time being.

About the 1st of September, 1927, Andrew Kalvik and Fred Peterson, white trappers of the district, hired Butch Smith to take them up the river to 20 miles above the Tik-chik River. They arrived one night at about 12 miles above the Tik-chik and camped for the night at a place called Harris Creek. Mr. Smith was awakened at 2 a.m. by a muffled cough. He got up and looked out the flap of the tent just in time to see a small dog appear from behind a clump of willows growing on the bank of the river, about 20 feet away, and no sooner had the dog appeared than a hand reached out and pulled the dog back from sight.

Mr. Smith awakened the other two men and together they kept watch for another sign of life. It was about an hour before a sign appeared and then it was a head or the top of the head of a man, as though he was going to look over the top of the willows. As soon as the head was seen Smith gave a yell and jumped and made a grab for the man. He was successful. He caught him by the forearm and pulled him into the tent, where a light was struck, and then they knew it was the crazy Indian Klu-tok.

He was not armed at the time, his rifle being in the skin boat, about ten feet away. He was held in the tent until morning. The three had decided to leave one man to watch the native and the other two to take the provisions up to the trapping ground, which would take about four hours. Harvey Kelvig decided to stay.

He was cautioned to keep good watch and not let the native get to his gun. The other two left and were gone about five hours, returning about noon. They landed at the place and Smith shouted "Here we are." However, they got no answer, and things began to appear different. They got out of the boat and went up to the tent, and there they found Kelvig shot through the arm and the back of his head cut open with an ax.

Evidently the native had got to his gun and shot at Kelvig, creasing him across the chin and knocking him down and finishing him with an ax. The native had fled and had taken his gun, ax, grub, and a few traps belonging to the trappers. However, he left his skin boat.

Neither Smith nor Peterson were armed, so they returned at once to report to the marshal. Smith swore out a complaint, and the commissioner and marshal left together with a coroner's jury for the scene of the murder. The inquest was held and the jury decided that foul play of some kind was the cause of his death and that the Indian Klu-tok was most likely responsible for the death.

Kelvig was buried where he fell.

Jack Aho went back and wintered in the upper reaches of the Nushagak River, about a mile above the Chu-chit-nok River. Sometimes in December Aho visited Sid Lohr in his cabin at the mouth of the King Salmon River, about four hours walk from the Aho cabin, and at that time Lohr told him he would call on him as agreed on, the Ist day of January, 1928. He called, and Aho was gone, having evidently just left that morning, because there was fresh bread and other things to show someone had been there recently. Lohr stopped there that night. Leaving a note, he returned to his own cabin the next day.

About the 1st of March Lohr visited Aho's upper cabin, about 35 miles up the river. Thinking Aho was trapping somewhere in the area, Lohr did not report him missing. Now that the trappers are all down with their beaver and other fur, Aho has not turned up. Natives stopped at Aho's upper cabin but stated that nothing had been touched in the cache. Evidently Aho has not been there since leaving his other cabin. It is now forty days past time for him to show up on the lower river, and he has not shown up. It is assumed that Klu-tok killed Aho.

Unless something is done at once to apprehend Klu-tok, the entire district here will have to be abandoned and the Indian given supreme command of the entire region.

AFTERWARD: Klu-tok's murderous career ended in 1931. In June, United States Deputy Marshal Stanley Nichols found dead in a cabin at the head waters of the Mulchatna River, a tributary of the Nushagak. As far as Nichols could determine, Klu-tok died of natural causes.

It is the view of this writer that "The man from the Mountain" was killed by white trappers or Indians, to avenge the deaths of friends and to make the country safe to trap. Marshal Nichols knew Justice had been served-- frontier style!

he Rat River trapper remains one of the enigmas of the northwestern frontier. He seemed to be a man without a past. Even his name, Albert Johnson, was in question. George Adit, a Cassiar trapper, claimed he knew Johnson as Arthur Nelson, a prospector who followed the gold rush into the Dease Lake country in 1924. Adit said he recognized Johnson from a picture in *True Detective Mystery Magazine*

However, the only documented picture of Johnson is a picture taken after his death, his features distorted in a death grimace.He may never be identified. But he will live in the legends of the North country as "The Mad Trapper of Rat River"-- the man who defied the Mounties for 54 days and died fighting to the end.

THE MAD TRAPPER OF RAT RIVER

Johnson drifted into the Northwest Territories of Canada in July 1932, camping near Fort McPherson. Shortly after arriving, he put on a shooting exhibition with automatic pistols. With a pistol in each hand, firing simultaneously, he shot away the target, a stake driven into the ground. Awed by the shooting, the Indians spread the word of Johnson's prowess with weapons.

Perhaps this was Johnson's intent-- a not so subtle threat to stay out of his territory. The story may have exaggerated his shooting prowess, but events soon proved Albert Johnson to be a deadly foe in a shoot out.

At McPherson he purchased an outfit and set out for Rat River. On a bend in the river, Johnson built a cabin and began trapping that winter. In December 1932, William Nerysoo, an Indian trapper, complained to the

ALBERT JOHNSON
Sketch by Alaska State Troopers

Mounties that Johnson was trapping without a license and tampering with Indian traps.

A Royal Canadian Mounted Police patrol was dispatched to Rat River to investigate the complaint. On December 26, 1931, Constables King and Bernard left Arctic Red River for the two day trip by dog sled. In the afternoon of the second day, the mounties stopped the team in the brush along the edge of Johnson's clearing. A strange sight met their eyes, a log cabin only four feet high squatted in a clearing near the river. Cautiously, King approached the cabin, calling out:

"Albert Johnson--Constable King of the Mounted Police. I would like to talk to you."

Later when he made his report to his commanding officer, King wrote: " I spent nearly a half of an hour at the cabin of Albert Johnson, knocking on the door and calling out to Johnson. Several times I informed him who I was and that I wished to speak to him. Yet he refused to open the door or answer. He made no response of any kind. But he was there. Once I saw him peeping at me through a small window near the door, which he immediately closed when he saw me looking at him."

Angry and frustrated, they returned to Aklavik sub-district headquarters for further instructions. Inspector Eames issued a warrant. King and Bernard, accompanied by officers McDowell and Lazarus Sittichiulis, made the eighty mile returned to Johnson's Cabin, the temperatures hovering around 40 degrees below zero.

In late morning of the following day, December 31st, the patrol approached the cabin. King shouted: "Mr. Johnson are you there ? Mr. Johnson, we have a warrant to search your place." Receiving no answer, King knocked on the door and identified himself. Without warning, Johnson fired through the door, hitting the mountie in the chest. King fell into the snow badly wounded. Immediately, the patrol opened fire. Under the covering fire, King struggled to his feet and staggered away from the cabin. Constable McDowell ran forward and helped King out of the line of fire. Johnson returned fire from a series of loop holes at the base of his cabin.

Breaking off the attack, the patrol started the long mush back to Aklavik to get medical aid for King, a trip made under extreme hardship. Snow had drifted over the trail, and the Mounties broke trail again--bone weary work on part of the men and dogs. The trail crossed and recrossed the frozen Husky River. The sled carrying Constable King had to be muscled over the river bank and around hummocks. Having already run nearly 40 miles that day, the dogs were exhausted. With temperatures ranging 40 to 50 degrees below zero, the patrol made the return trip in 18 hours.

Inspector A.N. Eames organized a posse to take Johnson dead or alive. He took nine men with him. Later Constable Edgar Millen and Charlie Rat, an Indian guide joined them at Blake's Post.

The Globe (Toronto) in its January 14, 1932

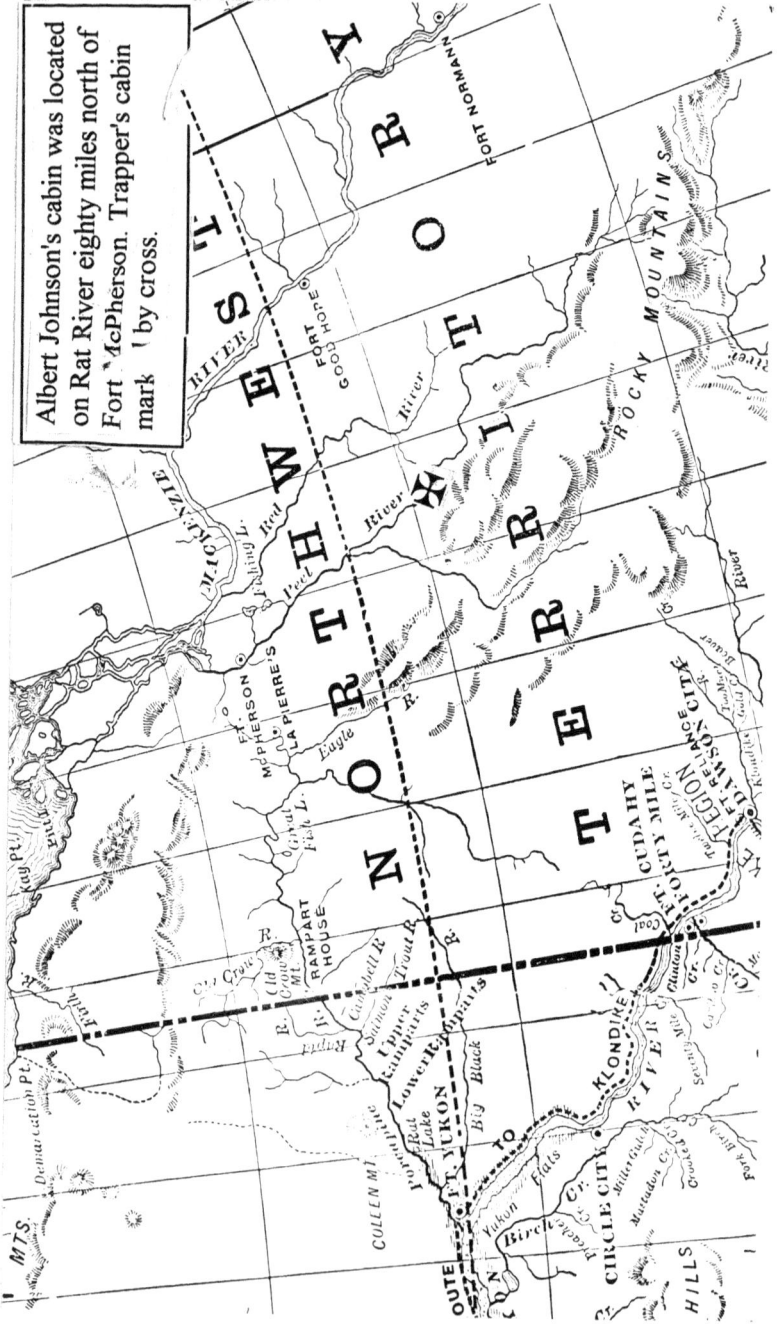

Albert Johnson's cabin was located on Rat River eighty miles north of Fort McPherson. Trapper's cabin mark by cross.

edition carried the story of the third assault on Johnson's cabin. [credit: The Canadian Press]

Mounted police at Aklavik laid plans tonight for the capture of the hermit trapper whose gunfighting from his lonely cabin has staved off two attempts to arrest him.

A report received at Royal Canadian Mounted Police headquarters here today told of a futile raid by eight Mounties on the cabin of Albert Johnson, wanted for the shooting of Constable A. W. King more than a week ago.

The police posse attacked Johnson's stronghold for fifteen hours with bombs and gunfire, and were forced to retire when their food supply ran low.

The party was headed by Inspector A. N. Eames of the Aklavik Division of the Royal Canadian Mounted Police. They left for Johnson's cabin eight days ago. When they reached his isolated hut, set on a brush covered promontory twenty miles upstream from the mouth of the Rat River, Johnson, believed to be demented, defied the contingent to arrest him.

In either hand he had an automatic pistol, and a shower of bullets greeted the Mounties as they sought to rush the cabin. Then Johnson retired inside the frame shack and fired at his assailants from loopholes in the walls. The attackers had difficulty working in the twilight of the Arctic night.

When the police party hurled high explosive bombs at the cabin, Johnson moved into a tunnel dug beneath his home. He was apparently prepared for this form of assault. Periodic rushes failed as the trapper fired through the loopholes.

During the attack members of the posse caught a glimpse of the cabin's interior. They said the floor was five feet below the ground level. Loopholes were at each corner of the shack, giving command of all sides of the building.

The report received here did not say how large a posse will be sent to dislodge the trapper. It will work from a base on the mouth of Rat River, where supplies will be kept.

After the last bundle of dynamite was hurled at the cabin and blew off the roof and most of the walls, Inspector Eames and Karl Gardland charged the cabin. Garland attempted to shine a flashlight through the door. A shot from the wrecked cabin knocked the flashlight from the Mountie's hand. Surprised the trapper was still able to fight, the patrol retreated to the river bank.

At 50 below, men could not last long without shelter. The cold and lack of supplies caused the Mounties to withdraw. Inspector Eames had not counted on the stubborn resistance put up by Johnson. The drop in temperature and dwindling supplies worried the Inspector and he ordered a retreat to Aklavik, arriving there on January 12.

On the 14th, Eames sent Constable Edgar Millen back to Rat River to watch Johnson, accompanied by the trapper, Karl Gardlund. Eames outfitted and organized another assault. On January 16, the group began the 80 mile trip to Rat River.

The *Edmonton Journal* for February 19, 1932 reported the final act Albert Johnson's life. The story was related by Q.M.S. Riddell of the Royal Canadian Signals.

"Upon arrival at Johnson's cabin on the 19th of January, we found that he had deserted the cabin and taken to the bush. Heavy snows had obliterated his trail and it became a question of covering the surrounding country in an attempt to pick up his tracks. As sufficient supplies for the whole party could not be carried by dog teams, Inspector Eames decided to leave four men, Constable Millen, R.C.M.P., two trappers, Gardlund and Verville, and myself, to carry on the search; and one man, S. Sgt. Hersey, at the base camp which was located close to Johnson's cabin. Sufficient supplies were left to maintain this smaller posse, and the others returned to Aklavik for additional supplies.

"Owing to the deep snow and heavy underbrush in

this country, together with the very short period of daylight at this time of year, locating Johnson's trail was a difficult and tedious matter, and it was not until eleven o'clock on the morning of January 30 that we overtook the fugitive. He had apparently paused for rest and had dug himself in a well protected triangular hole in a clump of brush.

"Immediately upon sighting him, Gardlund took a snap shot at him, and Johnson appeared to have been hit and fell back below the top of the barricade. As a precaution, we waited over two hours, during which time there was no sign of movement behind Johnson's improvised shelter.

"Believing him to be dead or seriously injured, the party then advanced. When we were within about 25 yards, Johnson suddenly sprang up and fired on us, hitting Constable Millen, and then dropped back out of sight. His position gave him the advantage and it was useless to try to advance further.

"We carried Millen out of the danger area but he expired within a few minutes. I got his rifle from where it had fallen in the snow when he was shot.

"As I had the fastest dog team, it was decided that I should 'mush' back to Aklavik to report Millen's death and to get additional men. I stopped at the base camp to send up Hersey to take my place. I got into Aklavik the next afternoon, Sunday. Inspector Eames broadcast a call for volunteers over the local broadcasting station, UZK, to which a number of trappers in the vicinity responded the next day. Inspector Eames also wired requesting that a plane be sent in to assist in the search, and to carry supplies as a great deal of time was lost in having to send men and dog teams back for supplies continually.

"On Tuesday morning the third posse left Aklavik under command of Inspector A.N. Eames, going in by way of Fort McPherson where we picked up additional volunteers. Owning to heavy winds and blizzards, the going was very rough and we had to break trail for the dogs practically all the way and we did not reach the point where Johnson was supposed to be encamped until late Saturday.

"We received word that night over our portable radio that Capt.W.R. "Wop" May of the Canadian Airways, accompanied by Constable William Carter, R.C.M.P. of Edmonton, would be over the area on Sunday. The plane arrived, and after circling several times, landed close to the forward party. "Wop" reported that apparently our man had fled as he had seen a faint trail leading from the barricade away into the divide.

"I was taken up in the plane to assist in tracing the trail. At one place a trail led off, heading directly for the divide, and also another trail, just as fresh looking, continued on up the creek but ended abruptly. Later on, we discovered a faint trail continuing on from this and ending in a circle.

"Evidently Johnson had circled back on his own trail and camped for the night just off his main trail so that he could watch it. A heavier, or fresher, trail led from this to his trail back along the creek as though he had back-tracked. After about an hour, we landed and reported to Inspector Eames. As a result, the base camp was moved up to the junction of the two trails.

"A party of us went ahead to examine the trails on the ground. This was the start of more than a week's hard grind of following Johnson's trails. The aeroplane made several attempts to cover the trail from the air, but the heavy winds which at times blew the drifting snow as high as a thousand feet, prevented the plane from making observations and also from being able to land and connect with the ground party until late in the week. By this time we had followed the trail backwards and forwards into the divide, and it was quite apparent that Johnson was attempting to get across to the Yukon side. The tracks indicated that he was growing groggy although, as he had a number of days start on us, he might have had a chance to rest since those tracks were made.

"On Friday Constable Sid May of the Old Crow detachment of the R.C.M.P. on the Yukon side, reported to Inspector Eames that Johnson had been seen in the vicinity of the Bell River on Wednesday. On Saturday morning Inspector Eames, Gardlund, and myself flew over to La Pierre House while the other party, including S.Sgt. Hersey [of the Canadian Army], continued on by dog team through the divide. The tracks did not look fresh, denoting that Johnson was some distance ahead but apparently was keeping in the vicinity of Bell River. Instead of continuing on his trail, the party decided to cut overland to shorten the distance.

"The forward party was joined late Monday by the party which had come over the divide by dog team. Close to La Pierre house, the traveling was difficult as the snow was very deep, but farther on the trails became excellent, being hard packed due to the thousands of caribou in the region.

"Early Wednesday morning, a party under Inspector Eames, including Constable May, Staff. Sgt. E.F. Hersey, Verville, Gardlund, an Indian special, Frank Jackson of La Pierre House, an Indian from Aklavik, and Peter Alexei, a local Indian who knew the district well, and myself, left camp which was about 25 miles from LaPierre House to follow Johnson's trail up the Eagle River. The trail was fairly good, though two days old. Gardlund and myself were making and setting out markers so the aeroplane could follow our route.

"As he had done several times before, Johnson doubled back on his own trail and we came upon him unexpectedly in a very crooked stretch of the river. Hersey with his team was in the lead, followed closely by Joe Verville.

"Johnson must have spotted Hersey a moment before Hersey saw him as when first seen, Johnson was running to the edge of the bank on the inside of a bend for cover. Hersey grabbed his Lee Enfield off the toboggan and ran to the centre of the creek where he would have a good

This drawing shows the desperate struggle in which Albert Johnson came to the end of the fugitive trail in the various stages to the final dramatic moment when he was cornered and hammered to death in a blast of rifle fire. The dotted line coming from the horizon shows the trail originated by Johnson and followed by the police posse. While Staff Sergeant Earl Hersey and trapper Joe Verville were at point marked "A," they suddenly saw Johnson at "1" and who was coming back on his own trail in preparation for back-tracking. Hersey who was close to the far bank of the creek, ran out to the centre at "B" to see Johnson better and the latter darted back to the bank at "2." Verville ran up to "C." and then Johnson began firing, striking Hersey while the latter was still at "B." Johnson then turned and fled while the other members of the posse raced to close with him. Hit in the leg, Johnson fell at point "3," put his packsack in front of him and kept shooting until bullets from the posse ended his life. *Edmonton Journal*, February 19, 1932.

view of Johnson. Verville following him.

"Johnson immediately opened fire from fairly good cover on the two boys in the centre of the creek, wounding Hersey as he knelt on one knee, firing. The rest of the party immediately scattered, some to the tops of the banks on either side of the creek, and some down the centre of the creek. Johnson started running back along his own trail, up the creek amidst a hail of bullets. He was knocked down from a distance of 500 yards, probably wounded in the leg. He then laid prone on the snow, and putting his large pack in front of him, commenced digging down in the deep, soft snow; the posse meanwhile rapidly overtaking, and partially surrounding him.

"Johnson fought desperately to the end, emptying his rifle, and was in the act reloading it when killed. The accurate shooting of the posse had riddled his body with bullets.

"The aeroplane had arrived overhead and landed as soon as the firing ceased. I dashed over to Hersey followed by the rest of the party, and to my joy found he was still alive. It at first appeared that he had been hit three times as he was bleeding from the knee, the arm, and the chest. However, it was later found that one bullet had caused all three wounds. As Hersey was kneeling on his right knee with his left elbow resting on his left knee, the bullet had grazed the knee cap, entered the elbow, came out the upper arm, and into his chest.

"First aid was immediately given and we carried Hersey to the aeroplane which took off at once. I accompanied my pal and inside of an hour and a half he was in the hospital in Aklavik under the care of Dr. Urquhart."

AFTERWARD: Ironically, pilot W.R. May transported Johnson's body to Aklavik in the same plane that was used in hunting the trapper. For several days, the body hung in a shed while the Mounties tried to identify him.

113

He was buried in the Aklavik cemetery.

Any of Johnson's effects having historical value were given to the Royal Canadian Mounted Police to be displayed in their museum in Regina, Saskatchewan. Included in this collection: a Savage lever action 30-30 rifle, Iver Johnson 16 gauge sawed off shotgun, and a Winchester 22 with a sawed off stock.

Alfred King recovered from his wounds and returned to duty, retiring in 1953. Staff Sergeant Earl Hersey's wound was not as serious as it first appeared to be. Apparently, he returned to his unit, the Signal Corps of the Canadian Army.

$\mathcal{I}$n 1898, stampeders packed over the Chilkoot and White Pass trails in never ending lines of people, animals and equipment. The trails wound through narrow canyons, bottlenecks that often stopped traffic--favorite spots for Soapy Smith's card sharks and shell game operators. They worked the crowd as the gold rushers waited for the trail to clear. Most men who fell prey to the nimble hands of the con men took their losses and moved on. For, If they complained, they were threatened and bullied by gang members. But in the winter of 1898, one man fought back--history does not record his name.

Glen Bushee witnessed the man's courage and slugging match that erupted into a gun battle. At the time, Bushee ran a packtrain carrying goods from Skagway over the White Pass to Lake Bennett. His account appeared in W.D.K. Weimer's *True Story of the Alaska Gold Fields* published in 1903.

GUN BATTLE ON THE WHITE PASS

"There were several pack trains going up the canyon, when we were about half a mile above the mouth of the canyon, we came to a stop because of some pack slipping off on one of the horses ahead. This threw quite a bunch of us together, men with sleds, men with packs on their backs and men with pack horses. There was a lot of horses in the crowd too.

"Very close to the trail was a gang of seven of Soapy Smith's shell game men, working their business. As I came up the racket with this man commenced. He had lost his money and turned to leave. When off a few feet, some of the gamblers yelled at him, jeering him very roughly for something he had said.

"The man was a good sized fellow and well built. He was dressed in a blue suit of mackinaws. He turned and replied grittily to the jeer. At this, one of the largest of the cappers squared off as if to strike the man in the blue suit. But quick as thought, the gambler was struck by the other and knocked down. Another gambler took a hand in the fight then, and he fell as quickly as the first fellow. The gamblers here, began to see that they had their hands full. A third one rushed into the fracas and would have met the same fate had he not been afraid of the skillful fists of the victim. The third one came into the fight by pulling his revolver and aiming at the man who was proving too much for the crowd.

"The spectators began to clear out about his time, but the trail was full and the canyon narrow, so there was no place much to go .

"As soon as the man in blue saw the gun in the hands of the gambler, he drew his own gun and backed off a step or two to get the seven enemies in line, and to get them in front of him. Then the shooting commenced. The gamblers commenced to hunt places of safety. They took refuge behind our pack horses and mules, and every man in the crowd, perhaps twenty five or thirty began to get into shelter from the bullets too. It was a scramble for life for everyone of us.

"The gamblers got their revolvers out as soon as they got behind their living breastworks and they began to fire at the man who was shooting at them. It was seven against one, and the seven protected by the horses and the one standing out in the open, apparently not caring whether he was hit or not, fired back. Every time he saw a head stick up, he would blaze away. One of the gamblers ran up to his tent and got a Winchester, and sighting it across the back of a mule blazed away at the man, but he missed him.

"The guns were blazing away on all sides. I was afraid my horses would be shot, but I was more afraid I would stop a bullet myself. The only shelter I saw was a hand sled loaded with goods. I ran to this and lay down on the ground to protect myself. I thought I was all right but some one yelled to me that I was in a dangerous place. I looked up and saw that one of the gamblers was firing directly in my direction. Then I noticed that the bullets might come in under the sled and hit me. I made a run for the trees, which I saw off to one side. I thought myself very lucky to get to them safely, but there were four or five men behind each one already, so we felt rather shaky. Two men were lying on the ground behind little stumps.

"The pack trains had scattered in all directions, and the gamblers found their breastworks moving away from them. The man in the blue suit, after emptying his revolver once, reloaded it coolly, and shot another round at the gamblers. This he did three times. I think that between forty and fifty shots altogether must have been exchanged. When the firing ceased, we came out of our hiding places and the gamblers quickly retreated down the canyon.

"There were many in the crowd of spectators who were just on the point of taking a hand in the battle, and helping the lone man out. If one man on the outside had opened with his revolver, there would have been no stopping until the entire seven men had been wiped out. It was a very narrow escape for them, I can tell you. The sympathy of the crowd was with the lone man, whose bravery was wonderful. As soon as it was over, there was talk of lynching the gamblers, and after some delay the men resolved to go down and string the fellows up.

"They got a rope and started down the canyon. The gamblers were nowhere to be seen. They had made good their escape. 'Soapy Smith' himself was not in the crowd himself and efforts to find out the name of fellow who gave the gamblers battle was unavailing."

𝓕rank Fuller drifted into the Coeur de Alene Mission of the Catholic Church in 1883. Learning that Father Tassi and Father Robault were joining Bishop John C. Seghers in Alaska to work among the Natives, Fuller asked to go along. The bishop agreed, thinking Fuller would prove a valuable asset to the expedition.

By the time the party reached Sitka on the steamer *Ancon*, Fuller showed signs of a disturbed personality. Alarmed, the priests begged the bishop to send the man back to Seattle. Bishop Seghers did not heed the warning, asserting that a trip away from civilization would be good for Fuller.

At Harper's Post on the Yukon, the missionaries parted. Reverend Fathers Tassi and Robault stopped at the post and the bishop and Fuller continued on to Nulato. In his diary, the prelate recorded instances of Fuller's deteriorating mental condition. He observed that Fuller at times became insanely enraged, violent and threatening.

At the last camp before Nulato, Fuller's mania apparently climaxed. An argument over a camping spot may have pushed Fuller over the edge. The following morning he awoke the bishop and shot him with a rifle.

The Alaska Free Press in its August 6, 1887 issue carried the story of Bishop Seghers' murder. Father Tassi relates the events leading up to the murder.

DEATH COMES FOR THE ARCHBISHOP

"It was a year ago last month," said Father Tassi, "that the bishop asked me to bring Frank Fuller with me to Alaska. I had known Fuller several years. He was a watchmaker in Portland for two or three years, but in 1881 he went to Washington territory. He came to the Coeur de Alene Mission, where I saw him in 1883. He went to Spokane Falls from there, and I met him with the Fathers at that place a year ago last March. He was very anxious to join me in my Alaska work, and asked several times to be allowed to go. The bishop told me to bring him along.

"We started from Victoria on the 13th of July a year ago, the bishop, Fuller and I. We went by steamer to Juneau. We then formed our party and went to Chilkat, from there, where we had our things carried across the mountains by Indians. We built a boat there and started down the Yukon. We arrived on the 7th of September at the mouth of Stewart river. Here, after a time, the bishop left me with another priest to carry on the work among the Stickeen Indians.

"The bishop, with Fuller and the Indians, proceeded down the river. We heard nothing more of them until we reached Fort Yukon, about the middle of June, and we then learned that the bishop was dead. From one of the Indian boys who was with Bishop Seghers, I learned the particulars of the murder.

"On the seventh day of the journey (it was the 27th of November), according to the boys' story, Fuller became morose and quarrelsome. They were about thirty miles from Noulata [Nulato]. Towards night Fuller asked the bishop to make camp. The bishop consulted the Indians, who advised against camping there and said that an Indian camp with a number of Indian houses could be found a few miles further on. The bishop told Fuller that the Indians knew better than they could, and he should follow their advice. Fuller claimed that more attention was paid to the Indians than to him. He talked so much about it that the Indians carried his words to the bishop. 'Never mind,' said the bishop, 'You know better than we.'

"They went on to the camp and made their bed. All slept together in a line. Fuller was the first to get up in the morning. He got some sticks ready for fuel, but sat down opposite the bishop without lighting them. The Indian at the end of the line rose and heard Fuller say, 'Bishop get up.'

"The bishop lifted his head and half rose when he saw Fuller with a rifle leveled at him. As Fuller fired, he clasped his arms across his breast and bowed his head. The bullet struck him squarely on the forehead and he never spoke. The muzzle was so close to him, that his face was powder-burned. All this happened so quickly that the Indian was not able to do anything. But when Fuller began to reload he sprang upon him and seized his gun, shouting to his companions that Fuller was going to murder them all.

"'No,' he says, 'I meant to kill only the bishop.'

"The Indians arranged the body as well as they could, and went with Fuller to Noulata. Fuller accompanied the body to St. Michael's and offered to give himself up. He confesses his crime freely, and cries about it. We have kept the witnesses at St. Michael's. They will appear at the trial."

AFTERWARD: Joseph B. Johnson, commissioner at Onalaska [Unalaska], asked Fuller why he killed Bishop Seghers. Fuller responded: "God told me to."

Fuller was taken to Sitka for trial. Before the trial he had admitted killing the bishop. But he told the court the shooting of the prelate was accidental. Fuller said he lifted his rifle to protect himself against one of the Indian guides who was attacking him with an axe, and the gun discharged killing the priest.

But, George Sneataw, testifying through an interpreter, said the shooting was deliberate. According to Sneataw, an argument broke out over a camping spot. Fuller wanted to camp, but the bishop would not permit it. He wanted to push on. Fuller became angry.

The next morning, November 27, 1886, Fuller awoke and asked the bishop what time it was. Seghers told him it was too early to get up, go back to sleep. A short time later, from about ten feet away, Fuller shot and killed the priest.

The inability of witnesses to express themselves in English probably worked to Fuller's benefit. The Native guides were the only witnesses to the murder, other than Fuller.

The jury was out 61 hours and took 19 votes--eight for first degree murder and four for acquittal. Unable to agree, the jurors compromised on a verdict of manslaughter.

Frank Fuller was sentenced to ten years in McNeil Island, a federal prison. For good conduct, his term was reduced. According to *The All Alaska Review* for October 1915, Fuller died a violent death after being released from prison, but the publication did not go into detail.

Archbishop Seghers' story has a supernatural twist. The Very Reverend P.F. Hylebos of Portland, Oregon experienced a vivid dream during the night of November 27, 1886. In the dream he saw Bishop Seghers shot and killed. Impressed with the strange occurrence, he noted the details in his diary. Later he learned the bishop had been killed and the dream accurately foretold the murder.

-1-

"The Unexpected" by Jack London is absolutely true. I met Mr. and Mrs. Nelson on board ship a few years ago when they were on their way south. They were going to some sanitorium for cure of rheumatism from which Mrs. Nelson

-2- was suffering. I think they are now living in Bellingham, Wash.

The Nelsons lived in Atlin for years, had a general store on one of the creeks— I think Birch creek

122

and they may have been
engaged in a small way
in mining.
I think they went to
Atlin the spring after

-3-
giving themselves up to the authorities in Juneau. there was no
trial, this was the spring following the ~~tradegy~~ tragedy.

M. B. Keller

(Mrs. Keller was the wife of Dr. Keller,
dentist, and old pioneer of Skagway,
Alaska) J.W.

"The Unexpected" by Jack London is absolutely true. I met Mr. and Mrs. Nelson on board ship a few years ago when they were on their way south. They were going to some sanitarium for cure of rheumatism from which Mr. Nelson was suffering. I think they are now living in Bellingham, Wash. The Nelsons lived in Atlin for a number of years, had a general store in one of the creeks--I think Birch Creek and they been engaged in a small way in mining. I think they went to Atlin the spring after giving themselves up to the authorities in Juneau. There was no trial. This was the spring following the tragedy.

Jack London's story in the August 1906 issue of *McClure's Magazine*, on the hanging of Michael Dennin [M.S. Severts] in Lituya Bay Alaska in 1899, caused wide controversy in the Territory. Miners claimed it did not happen the way London wrote it. True, London fictionalized the account, but the events were accurate.

The [Sitka] *Alaskan* in its October 13, 1906 issue carried an article on the authenticity of the story.

There are many people in Alaska who know the London's story, in the main, is a graphic description of the hanging of Severts at Lituya Bay in October 1899.

True there are some errors in the details, and the story is colored in many respects in order that the writer may make the heroine the leading character in the tragedy.

The man killed was Fragalia Stefano (Harkey) and the other man "Dutchy" who was wounded (but not killed, as London says) was Sam Christianson, the Juneau teamster.

Mr. and Mrs. Hans Nelson, the other two members of the party, are well known in Juneau and Douglas, for it was there the whole matter was reported to the government and all connected with the tragedy were exonerated.

Mrs. Nelson is an English lady reared in London England and all who know her say is just such a woman as London describes in his graphic pen picture in his fascinating story. Whoever told the story to London must have described Mrs. Nelson's character and disposition so minutely that the writer has attributed many acts to her in the tragedy that did not in fact occur in order that he might make more vivid her true self. Her maiden name was Hannah Butler, not Edith Whittlesy, as London says. Mr. and Mrs. Nelson now reside in Atlin.

Mr. Christianson gives the following version of the tragedy. "Mr. and Mrs. Nelson, M. S. Severts, and myself on the 6th day of October, 1899, were eating dinner in the cabin. Severts got thru eating and went out doors while the remainder of us remained at the table talking.

"In a short time he returned and opening the door leveled a 45 Colt's revolver at Stefano (Harkey) and shot him dead. Then he fired at me but the ball first struck a stone jar on the table then glancing, struck me in the back of the neck. I was so stunned that I fell to the floor, then he attempted to fire at Mrs. Nelson but her husband grasped his hand and suddenly jerking it down the gun was discharged the ball tearing an ugly wound in Severts' leg.

"Mrs. Nelson then sprang at him and throwing a towel or dish cloth around his neck choked him until Nelson overpowered him. He was then tied and every effort was made to signal a passing steamer but none stopped. Indians were hired to carry Severts four miles down to the lower cabin and there the natives guarded him for several weeks when he was tried and hanged.

"Severts himself begged to be killed and the Indians were present at the hanging. We all did everything in our power to have Severts explain to us why he wished to kill us but he would never say. When asked if it was for the money they had ($800 not $8,000 as London says), his only reply was 'may be.'

"There was never a cross word among us and it was the most 'unexpected' thing in the world. His confession admits that it was his intention to kill us all, take the money, and then report that the Indians had committed the crime."

During the gold rush, the only law in vast areas of the North was often administered by Judge Lynch and the Hanging Tree. Located hundreds of miles from the nearest law, miners convened courts, appointed judges, juries, and--if needed--executioners.

In 1906, *McClures Magazine* published a story by Jack London of frontier justice in Lituya Bay, Alaska. According to London's story, Edith and Hans Nelson executed Michael Denning for the murder of two of his partners in the winter of 1898. The story published in 1909, titled "The Unexpected,"was advertised as a true incident.

The Daily Alaskan (Skagway) in its May 2, 1900 issue referred to a hanging in Lituya Bay. The miners of the Lituya Bay Gold Mining Co. hanged Martin Sirvers for murder. The foreman of the mine was L.H. Nelson. London may have based his story on Nelson's account of the vigilante court and the execution of the miner.

Mrs. M.B. Keller, an early pioneer of Skagway, claimed she knew the Nelsons and that the account by London was true. In an undated, hand written note to the Alaska Historical Library, Mrs. Keller confirmed the authenticity of the story. The note is reproduced here and reader's can judge for themselves. London fictionalized the 1900 account, changing names as the Victorian writers were wont to do.

According to London, Edith Whittlesey was born in rural England in the 1870s. At an early age, she became a lady's maid and travelled with her employer to America. In Chicago, she met and married Hans Nelson, an immigrant from Sweden. After their marriage, Hans and Edith followed the mining strikes in Colorado, Dakotas, Idaho and British Columbia and on to Alaska.

A PRIVATE HANGING

The gold-seeking tide was flooding northward into Alaska, and it was inevitable that Hans Nelson and his wife should be caught up by the stream and swept toward the Klondike. The fall of 1897 found them at Dyea, but without the money to carry an outfit across Chilkoot Pass and float it down to Dawson. So Hans Nelson worked as a carpenter that winter in the outfitting-town of Skaguay.

The summer of 1898 found him and his wife threading the mazes of the broken coast-line in seventy foot Indian canoes. With them were their partners: "Dutchy," Michael Dennin, and Harkey. The Indians landed them and their supplies in a lonely bight of land a hundred miles or so beyond Lituya Bay, and returned to Skaguay.

First, spruce trees were cut down and a three room cabin constructed. To keep this cabin and to cook was Edith Nelson's task, for which she would receive an equal share of gold. The task of the men was to search for gold. They found a low-pay placer where long hours of toil earned each man between fifteen and twenty dollars a day. Taking advantage of good weather to work their claim, they delayed their return to Skaguay .

And then it was too late. Arrangements had been made to accompany several dozen local Indians on their fall trading trip down the coast. But, tired of waiting, the Indians had departed. There was no course left the party but to wait for transportation.

All went well. Their gold dust weighed up something like eight thousand dollars. The men made snow shoes, hunted fresh meat, and in the evenings played endless games of cards. Edith darned socks and mended clothes.

The Indian summer ended suddenly, and winter came. It came in a single night, and the miners awoke to howling wind, driving snow, and freezing water. Storm followed storm, and between the storms there was the silence, broken only by the boom of the surf on the desolate shore, where the salt spray rimmed the beach with frozen white.

All went well, until one morning they were waiting for Dennin to come in for breakfast. The door opened and Dennin came in carrying a shotgun.. All turned to look at him. Lifting the gun to his shoulder, Dennin fired twice. At the first shot Dutchy sank upon the table. Harkey jumped to his feet, at the second shot, and he pitched face down upon the floor, his "My God!" gurgling and dying in his throat.

Stunned, Hans and Edith sat at the table with bodies tense, their eyes fixed in a fascinated gaze upon the murderer. Dennin threw open the breech of the shotgun, ejecting the empty shells. Holding the gun with one hand, he reached with the other into his pocket for fresh shells.

He was loading the shells into the gun when Edith Nelson jumped up, distracting Dennin. Hans leaped on the man, knocking him to the floor. He was in a blind fury. Striding Dennin, he hit him with sledge-like blows, knocking him unconscious. Edith cried out for him to stop, grabbing his arm.

Hans staggered back against the wall, where he leaned, his face working in anger. Edith stood in the middle of the floor, gasping, her whole body trembling violently.

Dennin lay without movement. Partly under him lay the shotgun, still broken open at the breech. Spilling out of his right hand were the two cartridges which he had failed to put into the gun. Harkey lay on the floor, face downward, where he had fallen; while Dutchy rested forward on the table.

"My God, Hans" was Edith's first speech.

He did not answer, but stared at her with horror. Slowly his eyes wandered over the room, for the first time taking in its details. Edith bent over examining Dennin.

128

"Leave him alone," Hans commanded harshly in a strange voice. She looked at him in sudden alarm. He had picked up the shotgun and was thrusting in the shells.

"What are you going to do?" she cried, rising from her bending position. Hans did not answer, but she saw the shotgun going to his shoulder.

" He killed Dutchy and Harkey! and I am going to kill him."

"That's wrong," she objected. "There 's the law."

Hans sneered his incredulity of the law's potency in such a region. She argued and pleaded. Finally, Hans gave in.

"All right," he said. "Have it your way. And tomorrow or next day look to see him kill you and me. Better let me shoot him." Edith would not consent.

"At present we have two graves to dig," she said. "But first of all, we've got to tie up Dennin so he can't escape." They lashed Dennin, hand and foot. Then she and Hans went out into the snow. The ground was frozen. It was impervious to a blow of the pick. They first gathered wood, then scraped the snow away and on the frozen surface built a fire. When the fire had burned for an hour, several inches of dirt had thawed. This they shovelled out, and then built a fresh fire. Their descent into the ground progressed at the rate of two or three inches an hour.

It was hard and bitter work. The scurrying snow did not permit the fire to burn any too well, while the wind cut through their clothes and chilled their bodies. They held but little conversation. The wind interfered with speech. Beyond wondering at what could have been Dennin's motive, they remained silent, oppressed by the horror of the tragedy.

Four o'clock found the two graves completed. They were shallow, not more than two feet deep, but they would serve the purpose. Night had fallen. Hans got the sled, and the two dead men were dragged through the darkness and storm to their frozen sepulchre.

"Tomorrow, I will put up head-boards with their names," Hans said, when the graves were filled in. Edith was sobbing. A few broken sentences had been all she was capable of in the way of a funeral service, and now her husband was compelled to half-carry her back to the cabin.

Dennin was conscious. He had rolled over and over on the floor in vain efforts to free himself. He watched Hans and Edith with glittering eyes, but made no attempt to speak. They dragged him to his bunk and lifted him in.

"Better let me shoot him, and we'll have no more trouble," Hans said in final appeal. But Edith would not agree.

The murderer was a constant menace. At all times there was the chance that he might free himself from his bonds, and they were compelled to guard him day and night. The man or the woman sat always beside him, holding the loaded shot-gun. At first, Edith tried eight-hour watches, but the continuous strain was too great, and afterwards she and Hans relieved each other every four hours. As they had to sleep, and as the watches extended through the night, their whole waking time was expended in guarding Dennin. They had barely time left over for the preparation of meals and the getting of firewood.

Learning of the killing, the Indians had avoided the cabin. Hans went to their cabins to get them to take Dennin down the coast in a canoe to the nearest white settlement or trading post, but the errand was fruitless. Negook was head man of the little village, keenly aware of his responsibility.

"It is white man's trouble," he said, "not Siwash trouble. My people help you, then will it be Siwash trouble too."

He went back to the terrible cabin with its endless alternating four-hour watches. Sometimes, when it was her turn and she sat by the prisoner, the loaded shot-gun in her lap, her eyes would close and she would doze. Always she aroused with a start, snatching up the gun and swiftly looking at him.

She was preparing herself for a nervous breakdown, and she knew it. To add to the strain, she could not forget the tragedy. She remained as close to the horror as on the first morning of the killings. In her daily ministrations upon the prisoner, she was forced to grit her teeth and steel herself, body and spirit.

Hans was affected differently, becoming obsessed by the idea that it was his duty to kill Dennin; and whenever he waited upon the bound man, he jerked him around and cursed him. She would catch the two men glaring ferociously at each other, wild animals the pair of them-- on Hans's face, the lust to kill; in Dennin's, the fierceness and savagery of the cornered rat.

So Hans became another factor in the problem. At first it had been merely a question of right conduct in dealing with Dennin, and right conduct, as she conceived it, lay in keeping him a prisoner until he could be turned over for trial before a proper tribunal. But now entered Hans, and she saw that his sanity was involved. Nor was she long in discovering that her own strength and endurance had become part of the problem. She was breaking down under the strain.

After the third day, Dennin had begun to talk. His first question had been, "What are you going do with me?" And this question he repeated daily and many times a day. And always Edith replied that he would assuredly be dealt with according to law. In turn, she put a daily question to him, "Why did you do it?"

To this he never replied. Also, he received the question with outbursts of anger, raging and straining at the rawhide that bound him and threatening her with what he would do when he got loose, which he said he was sure to do sooner or later. At such times she cocked both triggers of the gun, prepared to meet him with leaden death if he should burst loose, herself trembling and palpitating from the tension and shock.

The days came and went. There was much of darkness and silence, broken only by the storms and the thunder on the beach of the freezing surf.

But in time Dennin grew more tractable. It seemed to her that he was growing weary of his unchanging recumbent position. He began to beg and plead to be released. He made wild promises. He would do them no harm. He would himself go down the coast and give himself up to the officers of the law. He would give them his share of the gold. He would go away into the heart of the wilderness, and never again appear in civilization. He would take his own life if she would only free him. His pleading usually culminated in involuntary raving, until it seemed to her that he was passing into a fit; but always she shook her head and denied him the freedom for which he worked himself into a passion.

But the weeks went by, and he continued to grow more tractable. And through it all the weariness was asserting itself more and more. "I am so tired, so tired," he would murmur. At a little later period he began to make impassioned pleas for death, to beg her to kill him, to beg Hans to put him out of his misery.

The situation was fast becoming impossible. Edith's nervousness was increasing, and she knew her breakdown might come any time. She could not even get her proper rest, for she was haunted by the fear that Hans would yield to his mania and kill Dennin while she slept.

Though January had already come, months would have to elapse before any trading schooner was even likely to put into the bay. Also, they had not expected to winter in the cabin, and the food was running low; nor could Hans add to the supply by hunting. They were chained to the cabin by the necessity of guarding their prisoner.

Something must be done, and she knew it. She knew that whatever she did she must do according to the law. It came to her that the law was nothing more than the judgment and the will of any group of people. Their collective judgment and will would be the law of that country. She was frightened at her own conclusion, and she talked it over with Hans. He added convincing evidence. He spoke of miners' meetings, where all the men of a locality came together and made the law and executed the law. There might be only ten or fifteen men altogether, he said, but the will of the majority became the law, and whoever violated that will was punished.

Edith saw her way clear at last. Dennin must hang. Hans agreed with her. Between them they constituted the majority of this particular group. It was the group-will that Dennin should be hanged. In the execution of this will, Edith strove earnestly to observe the customary forms, but the group was so small that Hans and she had to serve as witnesses, as jury, and as judges--also as executioners.

She formally charged Michael Dennin with the murder of Dutchy and Harkey, and the prisoner lay in his bunk and listened to the testimony, first of Hans, and then of Edith. He refused to plead guilty or not guilty, and remained silent when she asked him if he had anything to say in his own defense. She and Hans, without leaving their seats, brought in the jury's verdict of guilty. Then, as judge, she imposed the sentence. Her voice shook.

"Michael Dennin, in three days' time you are to be hanged by the neck until you are dead." Such was the sentence. The man breathed an unconscious sigh of relief, then laughed defiantly, and said, "Then I'm thinking the damn bunk won't be aching my back any more, an' that's a consolation."

With the passing of the sentence a feeling of relief seemed to communicate itself to all of them. Especially was it noticeable in Dennin. All sullenness and defiance disappeared, and he talked sociably with his captors, and even with flashes of his old wit. He also found great satisfaction in Edith's reading to him from the Bible. She read from the New Testament, and he took keen interest in the prodigal son and the thief on the cross.

On the day preceding that set for the execution, when Edith asked her usual question, "Why did you do it!" Dennin answered, "It's very simple. I was thinking --"

But she hushed him abruptly, asked him to wait. "Go," she told Hans, "and bring up Negook and one other Indian. Michael's going to confess. Make them come. Take the rifle along and bring them up at gun point if you have to."

Half an hour later Negook and Hadikwan were ushered into the death chamber. They came unwillingly, Hans with his rifle herding them along.

"Negook," Edith said, "there is to be no trouble for you and your people. Only is it for you to sit and do nothing but listen and understand." Thus did Michael Dennin, under sentence of death, make public confession of his crime. As he talked, Edith wrote his story down, while the Indians listened, and Hans guarded the door for fear the witnesses might bolt.

He had not been home to the old country for fifteen years, Dennin explained, and it had always been his intention to return with plenty of money and make his old mother comfortable for the rest of her days. "An' how was I to be doin' it on sixteen hundred?" he demanded. "What I was wantin' was all the gold, the whole eight thousand. Then I could go back in style. I would kill all of you and report it at Skaguay for an Indian-killin', an' then pull out for Ireland. And, that's my confession."

"Negook and Hadikwan, you have heard the white man's words," Edith said to the Indians. "His words are here on this paper, and it is for you to make a sign, thus, on the paper, so that white men to come after will know that you have heard."

The two Indians put crosses opposite their signa-atures, received a summons to appear on the morrow with all their tribe for a further witnessing of the hanging.

Dennin's hands were released long enough for him to sign the document. Then a silence fell in the room.

Hans was restless, and Edith felt uncomfortable. Dennin lay on his back, staring straight up at the moss-chinked roof. "An' now I'll do my duty to God," he murmured. He turned his head toward Edith. "Read to me," he said, "from the book."

The day of the execution broke clear and cold. The thermometer was down to twenty-five below zero, and a chill wind was blowing which drove the frost through clothes and flesh to the bones.

"I'm wishin' there was a priest," he said wistfully; then added swiftly, "But Michael Dennin's too old a campaigner to miss the luxuries when he hits the trail."

He was so very weak and unused to walking that when the door opened and he passed outside, the wind nearly carried him off his feet. Edith and Hans walked on either side of him and supported him. He arranged the forwarding of his share of the gold to his mother in Ireland.

They climbed a slight hill and came out into an open space among the trees, near a shallow grave Hans had burned the earth. Here circled solemnly about a barrel that stood on end, were Negook and Hadikwan, and all the Indians down to the babies and the dogs.

Dennin cast a practical eye over the preparations, noting the grave, the barrel, the thickness of the rope, and the diameter of the limb over which the rope was passed.

"Lend me a hand," he said to Hans, with whose assistance he managed to mount the barrel. Denning bent over so that Edith could adjust the rope about his neck. Then he stood upright while Hans drew the rope taut across the overhead branch.

"Michael Dennin, have you anything to say?" Edith asked in a clear voice that shook in spite of her. Dennin shuffled his feet on the barrel, looked down, and cleared his throat.

"I'm glad it's over with," he said. "You've treated me like a Christian, an' I'm thankin' you hearty for your kindness."

135

"Then may God receive you, a repentant sinner," she said..

He answered, "May God receive me, a repentant sinner."

"Good-by, Michael," she cried, and her voice sounded desperate. Hans shoved and the barrel went out from under Michael Dennin.

"Take me to the cabin, Hans," she managed to articulate. "And let me rest," she added. "Just let me rest, and rest, and rest."

With Hans' arm around her, supporting her weight and directing her helpless steps, she went off across the snow. But the Indians remained solemnly to watch the working of the white man's law that compelled a man to dance upon the air.

AFTERWARD: The Nelsons went to Juneau and reported the hanging, but no charges were brought against them. According to Mrs. Keller, the Nelsons ran a general store for several years in Atlin, British Columbia, but the *Polk's Directory* for 1905 did not list a Hans Nelson in Atlin.

MOLLIE WALSH, the wonder girl of White Pass Trail. Alone, and without help in the winter of 1897-8 she ran a tent road-house and fed and lodged the wildest and most persistent men Alaska ever saw and remained as clean morally as the snow that fell on her tent.

If there are still men on earth who ate Mollie's frugal meals, and were sheltered by her tent, let them thank their God for having had that lucky chance, for as sure and as long as snow falls on Alaska, Mollie Walsh will be remembered as the girl on whose headstone could be most fittingly inscribed:

HERE LIES DRAMA!
Mollie Walsh was murdered by her husband.
October 28th, 1902

$\mathcal{F}$or many years, a bronze bust of Mollie Walsh stood in the Pullen House garden in Skagway. Jack Newman, early day packer and gunfighter, erected the statue to Mollie in 1932. Jack met the comely Iowa girl when she was operating a grub tent near Log Cabin on the White Pass Trail.

According to legend, Jack had frozen his hands and stopped at Mollie's tent to thaw out. She massaged the packer's hands until circulation was restored. Jack later reminisced, "something passed between them" and he lost his heart to the girl and ardently pursued her. The courtship went well for awhile, but Mike Bartlett, another packer, began to pay attention to Mollie. Jack ordered her not to see Bartlett. In recalling the incident Jack said:

"Mollie was angry, for sure. She said I wasn't her master, not being married to her, and this was a public eating place, so everyone in the whole Northland was welcome. One thing led to another... Neither of us would weaken. Then Mollie up and married the skunk."

Mike Bartlett, a partner in Bartlett Bros. Packers and Forwarders, made a fortune packing supplies and equipment into the gold camps. He squandered the money on drinking bouts and bad investments. Beneath his rugged good looks, lurked a homicidal personality that liquor unleashed.

While living in Dawson, the Bartletts became close friends with another couple-- Jack Lynch and his wife. Jack and Mollie soon developed more than just a friendly interest in each other. Lynch, a business associate with Mike, fraudulently obtained power of attorney for the Bartlett business. While Mike was away on a trip to the creeks, Lynch mortgaged the Bartlett holdings, and along with Mollie and baby Leon departed Dawson on a sternwheeler.

Bartlett tracked the trio for the next several months. Apparently, Mollie and Jack lived in Seattle for awhile. In the fall 1901, Lynch returned to Dawson. The record is not clear, but Mollie probably stayed in Seattle. Perhaps the affair had cooled by that time.

Mike located his wife and son in Seattle, and the couple reconciled. Mike returned to Dawson, later followed by Mollie. After a short stay in the Yukon, she returned to Seattle to start a boarding house.

After settling his business affairs in Dawson and Nome, Mike returned to Seattle. At first he could not find Mollie; she had moved to a cheap rooming house, having closed the boarding house. Apparently, Mike visited Mollie and his son frequently, but did not live with them.

On October 28, 1902, Mike appeared at Mollie's room. Inflamed by liquor, he accosted his wife who lay sick in bed, their son lying next to her. Chasing the boy out of the bed, Mike pulled his revolver and threatened Mollie. She fled into the street. Mike chased after her, shooting her twice with a pistol, instantly killing her. *The Seattle Post-Intelligencer* in its October 28, 1902 edition printed the tragic account.

THE MURDER OF A FALLEN ANGEL

After repeated threats, Michael Bartlett shot and killed his wife last evening, and then attempted suicide. Two shots, one through the head and one through the breast resulted in the woman's death almost instantly. Bartlett, who injured himself but slightly, is in the county jail awaiting the course of the law.

The story is one of a pitiful struggle on the part of the wife. Bartlett's insatiable passion was for money with which to buy drink and to spend upon other pleasures. His wife was on the point of selling the furniture they possessed,which was all their worldly goods, that she might divide it with her husband, and with her portion leave him and care for herself and her child. To the police she said two weeks ago, that he abused her in all the ways which he could devise, called her all the names his nature could suggest, and had often threatened to kill her. She told the police officers, that Bartlett had in his day killed his man, though she alone beside him knew it, and that he was thoroughly desperate and criminal. She was advised to prosecute him by law and the next morning after his arrest swore to the complaint.

The woman with her little child lived in the back room of a house at 1426 Sixth avenue, and the husband spent much time there. They once lived on Seventh avenue and there the household furniture is still stored. They had moved to the little room, she said, as she did not care to live in a respectable place and submit to the treatment she was forced to endure.

In the front of the house the Klein family resides. Three rooms open straight back from the front door. Off the back room is the sleeping room in which Mrs. Bartlett was when the trouble began.

Bartlett left the house about 7 o' clock last night with the scornful jest that there might be something happening when he returned. In his absence the children of the Klein family were playing in the back room and in the bedroom where Mrs. Bartlett lay. To the eldest, Ethel, who gave a very clear story of the affair, she expressed the fear that her husband would kill her when he returned. She seemed greatly agitated and talked considerably to those about her. The little boy had been undressed and was in bed beside his mother, but a short while after they had finished their evening meal.

In about a half an hour the head of the family returned and roughly ordered the children to a front room.

"You had better go away; I can enjoy myself better without you" is the remark he is said to have made.

The children did as he had bidden them. He closed the bedroom door, and in a few minutes they heard a

140

great noise within the room. Screaming and waving her arms excitedly about her, the wife threw open the door and rushed toward the front of the house. The infuriated man ran close behind her, and as she entered the front room fired at her from behind. The bullet went close to its mark, and the smoke from the 45-caliber revolver burned the eyebrow of one of the little boys, who was running to get out of his way as he passed.

Quickly the two passed into the street, and there Bartlett fired two more shots in rapid succession. His victim stopped, reeled and fell. Then he fired two more shots, both at himself. The first evidently had no effect. The second grazed his scalp on the right side, making a flesh wound which will prove more painful than dangerous. He, too, fell, and it was thought by Mounted Patrolman Bannick, who was passing and saw that part of the affair, that the man had accomplished his own end. A cursory examination led to the belief that the wound might prove fatal, but when the man reached the hospital it was plain that he was but slightly injured.

"Did you shoot your wife?" was the question asked Bartlett as he regained consciousness. He shook his head. "Do you know she is dead and lying close beside you?" was another question.

"Is she?" he asked faintly, as he turned his head in an effort to see the woman who he had killed. His consciousness left him again on the way to the hospital, and when he said anything later it was to declare that he had nothing to do with the shooting, even of himself.

Many in the neighborhood heard the shots: some say there were four all together, and some say there were five. Several people ran to the place and lights were brought to illuminate the dark alleyway. The two bodies were found close together in the mud. The woman was clad only in her night garments.

After the shooting George Ferrell was one of the first to reach the scene. Cloths were placed over the bodies and the police and undertakers were summoned.

The body of the woman was placed in Butterworth & Sons' morgue, while the patrol wagon conveyed Bartlett to the hospital.

At the morgue it was found that two shots had passed through the woman's body, one through her head and one through her back. Both had been fired from behind as she ran. The one through the body, Coroner Hoye said, probably would have been fatal, but the other would not necessarily have been. The lower bullet entered the body underneath the right shoulder blade and ranged to the left, probably passing through the heart, and made its exit through the left breast under the nipple. The other bullet entered the head at the lobe of the left ear, passing downward through the mouth and outward above the jaw and through the upper lip. This is the wound which she might have survived. A peculiar feature of the latter shot was that a circular gold earring was hit squarely and broken by the bullet. A fragment was bent almost into the shape of a fish hook and the pointed end was carried far into the head.

Coroner Hoye will probably hold an autopsy on the body today. This may be postponed if Bartlett is not able to testify. In spite of the denials of Bartlett, the many witnesses declare that he and no other committed the crime. Late last night he could be heard to mutter dire threats against one "Shorty," but they were meaningless. It was learned however that Shorty was a man whom Bartlett knew by sight and who had been the first after the shooting to ask him for an explanation. To him Bartlett had returned nothing but shakes of the head. The man whose name Bartlett was muttering said he knew the murdered woman by sight, but had often seen the husband.

For two or three hours after the shooting took place the small house and the entrance to the alleyway were crowded with people desirous of learning the particulars of the tragedy. Patrolmen Melvin and Hadeen were sent to the place to render any assistance possible, and later, at the order of the Chief of Police Sullivan, Sergeant George Leighton went from headquarters to take charge of the effects of the couple and to see that the little child received attention. The back rooms of the house are scantily furnished, and in them are just the necessary utensils for cooking and living. The bureau drawers had in them the personal effects of the mother and child. In a trunk containing more articles of the mother were found the pictures of herself and her husband as well as of her little son.

The little boy Leon is a little more than two years of age. He was utterly bewildered by the awful events. He seemed to enjoy the ride to police headquarters in the arms of Sergeant Leighton. At the station he wandered about, occasionally setting up a plaintive cry for his mother. He was placed in charge of Police Matron Chapin who took him to her home.

Bartlett is well known to many Klondikers who were in the early rush. Since 1891 he has made at least $100,000, principally in the North. He packed over the old Dyea trail and the Skagway trail and latter carried on operations in the interior. He is a large good-looking man or at least he probably did not look desperate before he began excessive dissipation.

Mrs. Bartlett has been forced to look out much for the daily bread. She kept a lodging house for awhile, but was forced to discontinue this because the owner of the building raised the rent to a figure she was unable to pay. The landlord promised to find her another location. This has never been found, and at last the woman had given up hope and determined to sell the furniture in hopes of getting away from her husband. She planned to give him half. This she hoped, so she told the police, would satisfy for awhile his demands and would give her a chance to something for the support of herself and child.

Although the husband has not made his home with them, he came frequently and spent much time about there. His plea was that he wanted to see his child, and last evening carried to the house a package of candy.

The rooms occupied by the family were locked and for some time will be kept in their present condition, as further light may yet be thrown upon the tragedy.

AFTERWARD: At the trial, Bartlett's lawyer argued temporary insanity brought on by alcoholism and Mollie's infidelity. The jury acquitted Mike of murder, remanding him to a mental institution in Oregon. Two years later, he committed suicide.

Mollie Walsh Bartlett's body was sent to St. Paul, Minnesota for burial. She was thirty one years old at the time of her death. Very little is known about the son, Leon ("Leo"). He served in the First World War dying in the 1950s.

Jack Newman married a widow in Seattle, Washington and lived out his life there. But in his heart, he still loved a comely 19 year old girl that ran a grub tent on the White Pass Trail. A girl that Jack remembered "was as pure as the snow that fell on her tent."

He commissioned a bust of Mollie to be placed in Skagway. The sculpture was dedicated on July 21, 1932. Unable to attend the ceremony, Jack cabled: " My excuse for not being at the dedication is that I'm an old man and no longer suited to the scene, for Mollie is still young and will remain young forever. .. I only wish to say I am a better man a--better--citizen for having known Mollie Walsh. She influenced me always for good. Her spirit fingers still reach across the years and play on the slackened fingers of my old heart... in such sad undertone that only God and I can hear."

Jack Newman wanted to be buried on the White Pass Trail, but Mrs. Newman probably had enough of Jack's infatuation with Mollie Walsh and when he died, she buried him in Seattle.

Mollie's statue was moved closer to town. Immortalized in bronze, she remains forever the young girl Jack Newman fell in love with.

MOLLIE WALSH

ALONE WITHOUT HELP
THIS COURAGEOUS GIRL
RAN A GRUB TENT
NEAR LOG CABIN
DURING THE GOLD RUSH
OF 1897-1898
SHE FED AND LODGED
THE WILDEST
GOLD CRAZED MEN
GENERATIONS
SHALL SURELY KNOW
THIS INSPIRING SPIRIT
MURDERED OCT. 27
1902

About the Author

Ed Ferrell grew up in Arizona. In the late 1940's, he went to Alaska and worked at various construction jobs, and with the Alaska Road Commission surveying roads. Except for time "Outside" to get a degree in journalism, he has lived in Alaska. After college, Ferrell taught high school English in Southeastern Alaska. During the summers, he explored the gold rush country of Alaska and the Yukon. After retirement, he began researching and writing about Northern history.

Ferrell lives in Juneau, Alaska with his wife Nancy. He has a son, William and a daughter, Patricia.

Other books by Ed Ferrell:

Biographies of Alaska-Yukon Pioneers (Heritage Books, Inc.)

Three volumes in this series have been published. Each book contains over 400 biographies or obituaries taken from early day Alaska and Yukon newspapers. This work fills a void by making obscure and unindexed material available to researchers in Alaskan and Canadian history. The majority of these early Northlanders came to the Territories between 1889 and 1910.

Strange Stories of Alaska and the Yukon (Epicenter Press)

Stories of unsolved mysteries mostly gleaned from early day newspapers make up this collection from the Northland. Ghosts, lost civilizations, strange creatures, lost mines, and tropical valleys amid the glaciers are the focus of this collection. Among the most puzzling stories in this book are accounts of Aztec-like artifacts and strange coins uncovered during mining operations in the Yukon and western Alaska.

www.ingramcontent.com/pod-product-compliance
Lightning Source LLC
Chambersburg PA
CBHW050019100426
42739CB00011B/2717